STEEL IN THE BLOOD

RECKONING BOOK 1

N. T. NARBUTOVSKIH

NEW DEGREE PRESS

COPYRIGHT © 2021 N. T. NARBUTOVSKIH

All rights reserved.

STEEL IN THE BLOOD

Reckoning Book 1

ISBN	978-1-63730-817-2	Paperback
	978-1-63730-879-0	Kindle Ebook
	978-1-63730-971-1	Ebook

STEEL IN THE BLOOD

For You

This story wouldn't have been possible without the love and support of a great many people. First, to Evie and Sloane, who put up with endless discussions about the nature of power and what it means to be human, as well as my incessant practice reading before bed. To Abby, my partner in all things, whose fearless and surgical editing kept me walking the fine line between Dickens and Hemingway. To Jared, who can reveal the best core of the worst possible writing. To Christina, Andrew and Yoon Ha, whose pathfinding and feedback gave me the confidence to put this story down in the first place. And to all those listed below, who took an idea and forged it into reality. To the faithful readers and early supporters, this is your story, and now, your book.

Adam Dunn
Alexander Biegalski
Amber Dawson
Anna Narbutovskih
Bartholomew W Clark
Benjamin Sides
Bradley Henicke
Brie Van Cleave
Chris Magdalenski
Christopher Phillips

Courtney Barger
Dan Wright
Dane Coppini
Dave Blair
Ellen Habermacher
Emily Short
Eric Koester
Geoff Habermacher
George Salloum
Graydon Sponaugle

Alex Moon
Ian Boley
Ian Crawford
Ian Sean Wolfe
Ian Teegarden
J Brandon Hicks
Jacob Meins
James Eichelberger
Jana Giraud
Jason Depew
Jason Womack
Jeff Gray
Jehon Bendokas
Jeremiah Williams
Jessica Brown
Joey Dumas
John Campion
John Connelly
John Galbreath
Joseph Schaefer
Joshua Newman
Joshua Stinson
Juan Ramirez
Laura Barger
Lillian Greene
Maria Korolov
Mark Jacobsen
Matt Sabatino
Matthew Voke

Megan Allison
Meredith Young
Nathan McClure
Pat & Beth O'Grady
Paul Kitko
Raul Roldan
Rosemarie Wilde
Ross P. Shober
Ryan Natalini
Samantha Lang
Sarah Brehm
Sarah Mashburn
Sarah McWilliams
Sasha Barrionuevo
Scott 'Mad Dog' Siler
Scott Nakatani
Sean Krassow
Shari Jean Hafner
Simon Mace
Stephen Davis
Steven Prosser
Steven Shultz
Suresh Yalamanchili
Tara Jernigan
Theresa Dumont
Thomas Outlaw
Tony Weedn
Victoria Barger
Vincenza Grossman

CONTENTS

	PROLOGUE	11
CHAPTER 1.	IN WHICH THERE IS A SLAUGHTER	17
CHAPTER 2.	IN WHICH THERE IS FENCING	25
CHAPTER 3.	IN WHICH THE DEAD ARE WOKEN, SORT OF	31
CHAPTER 4.	IN WHICH THERE ARE MACHINATIONS	39
CHAPTER 5.	IN WHICH AN UNEVENTFUL BREAKFAST HAPPENS	47
CHAPTER 6.	IN WHICH PLANS ARE LAID	53
CHAPTER 7.	IN WHICH DEEDS AND WORDS COLLIDE	63
CHAPTER 8.	IN WHICH LOVERS MEET	71
CHAPTER 9.	IN WHICH THERE IS TREASON	75
CHAPTER 10.	IN WHICH MEN DIE	81

CHAPTER 11.	IN WHICH ALL IS LOST	89
CHAPTER 12.	IN WHICH ALL IS NOT LOST	95
CHAPTER 13.	IN WHICH AN OLD EVIL ARISES	99
CHAPTER 14.	IN WHICH THERE ARE UNCOMFORTABLE TRUTHS	107
CHAPTER 15.	IN WHICH PLANS ARE LAID FOR WAR	115
CHAPTER 16.	IN WHICH A TORCH IS PASSED	125
CHAPTER 17.	IN WHICH THERE ARE GUNS	129
CHAPTER 18.	IN WHICH THERE IS A STOWAWAY	135
CHAPTER 19.	IN WHICH THERE IS REBIRTH	143
	INTERLUDE	149
CHAPTER 20.	IN WHICH SHADOWS ARE CAST	151
CHAPTER 21.	IN WHICH SPARKS FLY	155
CHAPTER 22.	IN WHICH WAYS PART	159
CHAPTER 23.	IN WHICH MEAD IS DRUNK	163
CHAPTER 24.	IN WHICH THERE IS A BEATING	169
CHAPTER 25.	IN WHICH MORE MEN DIE, AND ONE WOMAN	175

CHAPTER 26.	IN WHICH	
	THERE ARE WHISKEY AND NAMES	181
CHAPTER 27.	IN WHICH	
	THERE IS TRUTH	189
CHAPTER 28.	IN WHICH	
	PLANS ARE REMADE	193
CHAPTER 29.	IN WHICH	
	THERE ARE RATS	199
CHAPTER 30.	IN WHICH	
	THE RATS ARE NOTICED	203
CHAPTER 31.	IN WHICH	
	THERE ARE WARRIORS	205
CHAPTER 32.	IN WHICH	
	THERE MAY BE COMBAT	213
CHAPTER 33.	IN WHICH	
	STRANGE THINGS ARE FOUND	219

PROLOGUE

She came into the world naked and omniscient. The thin bones of her forearm seemed featherweight, nearly translucent in the gloaming. The light came from everywhere, bathing the base of the tree in luminescence. She clucked, thoughtful, as she turned her hand back and forth, flexing her fingers and watching sinew slide over bone. Delicately, she dropped her arm and began to walk the path before her. Behind her, the tree's hollow that had birthed her spread open, a mother-tree, its roots plunging into the frozen ground. Above, the great branches spread golden fingers across the grey sky. Its gnarled limbs twisted and turned, sharply and with purpose, pressing out farther and farther into the mist until they were lost from view. Though her breath clouded the air before her and her feet crunched on frozen leaves, the tree bore summer foliage. She smiled, taking it all in as she spun a slow circle while she followed the path.

It led her farther from the base of the tree, curling through a heather hedge. As she walked, the silence struck her. Nothing moved, save her. The path turned and looped, now promising to open up and then the hedges flowing back in, nearly meeting overhead in a dead brown and impassible wall. For the longest time, the only sound was her gentle breath and the soft fall of her feet, now cold and prickling like the ground. Then, carried through the crisp air ahead of her on the scent of burning leaves, she heard a steady clicking and smiled.

The sound grew louder as she followed the path. She suddenly came to a clearing, the hedge ending as if parted by a pane of glass. Ahead of her, the ground sloped down. The grass trampled around a low circle of stones.

She walked closer, catching sight of the source of the sound. "An auspicious manifestation. Shall I call you sisters?"

The two women she addressed turned from the loom set beside the well, one of middling age holding yarn on a spindle while the other's gnarled hands flickered back and forth. The shuttlecock blurred as the loom worked. The old weaver let a wry smile creep up the corners of her mouth, her eyes fixed on her work.

"That feels right, given the surroundings. I thought it appropriate, given our…" Here the weaver paused. "Mutual problem."

She walked down to stand beside the two at the loom. "So, who's who in this little metaphor of yours?"

The older woman snorted. "I think that's obvious."

She smiled, knowing as last to arrive, she had the least say in her manifestation. "I suppose you expect me to play along then. Pleased to meet you, wise old woman."

The elder laughed fully this time. "Old! Hah. Old. Look at you, not ten minutes in a young body and already impertinent."

The middle woman sighed, her face a mask. "If it's not too much trouble, I'd very much like to get on with this nonsense. You two are lucky I humor your ridiculous obsessions with anachronism."

Now it was the youth's turn to snort. "Simply because you don't see the importance in meaning and metaphor doesn't mean that importance doesn't exist. Don't fight the process. Besides, we aren't here to bicker amongst ourselves."

The old woman nodded, her eyes back on the loom, blur after blur as her hands and feet worked. "True enough. We need to talk about them."

The middle woman sighed again but remained silent. The other two knew her mind. It was to be the youth that spoke.

"You know it's worth a chance. They have been severed from us a long time, perhaps too long, but perhaps not. We cannot simply let them go."

The older woman clucked and shook her head once sharply. "You knew them as well as I did. They'll be full of grand schemes, some wayward faith in the nature of humanity. We all saw what that got us."

"That was a long time ago, as you said yourself. They might be able to shake the humans loose from the Empress."

"And what good can a single person do? They've been out of touch for too long. If they could change something, change anything, they would have by now. No, they've found some reason to stay. They always had an obsession with the humans."

"Obsession? Is that what you think?"

"What else can you call it?"

"Love."

"Love! Hah. Don't speak to me of love. Setting aside this old body, you don't know what that word even means. What about the love for their own kind? What about the love for life and freedom and all the things we hold dear? Where is their love for that?"

The young woman stamped her foot, the cold sending needles up her leg. "You know they love us just as we love them. How could they not? We are all so close to each other. We don't have a choice, really. We must love. But is that love? Is it love when you can't choose it?"

"Don't be dramatic. I think you're living into that youthful body too much."

"You haven't answered my question."

The old woman looked up from her weaving. "I don't need to."

"You've seen who they're with. There's a chance, albeit a slim one. Perhaps they can change him."

"And what good would changing a single human do? No good at all."

"You're wrong. All it takes is one human to see. Have you given up hope?"

The older woman sighed, and the blazing shuttlecock came to a stop in her hand. "What color is this?"

"Grey."

"That's right, grey. I can weave with all my skill, tighten every row, put this grey thread precisely in place. I can do everything to make this thread as best as it can possibly be. But it'll never be a golden thread."

"Really? Wyrd? That's the explanation you have for your despair?"

The elder woman nodded, beginning her weaving again. "Of course. The same way as you'll never be a human, neither will they, as much as they'd like to be. And the man will never see. Never change. It's the way of it."

The young woman glanced to the middle one, who had stood tight-lipped holding the skein of thread. Her youthful fingers reached out and touched the thread, gently running down the tightly coiled mass. The middle woman tried to move the skein away but was too slow, and everywhere the young fingertips touched, pools of brightness spread, the thread shifting and shimmering as it flowed into liquid gold.

The young woman's voice was no longer high and clear. The now deep sound cut through the crisp air of the manifestation with the hum and rattle of eons.

"Humans are not thread, dear sister. We shall see."

1

IN WHICH THERE IS A SLAUGHTER

———

Hear thee, oh reader mine
And heed the tale I tell
Once in the Highest Hall
Did the Old One seek wisdom

The old man poured forth truth, and the boy drank it in. The corners of the old man's wizened eyes held a glimmer of tenderness, despite his stern expression, as he regarded the youth. They were the shocking green of a wine-dark sea, the green of a jungle canopy that shouted life against the dead grey and silver of the room. They shone as emeralds above the red and gold brocade of his ceremonial vacuum suit, its cloak pinned with golden crescents of the Geneline Obershire. The fold was soon, but he had a few minutes to mentor the boy, who looked up at him with eyes the mirror image of his own.

"And what do you remember of the system, the star we circle?"

The boy's answer was a mantra, the words recited without the completeness of understanding beneath them. "The star is red, like so many others. We circle it and draw from it to fold and keep the schedule. We work on the flat, tune the array, and all of humanity relies on us."

The old man nodded, the barest smile curling the corner of his mouth. "Yes, all of that is true. But what does it mean?"

The boy frowned, his brows furrowed. "I heard some of the older kids talking in Basic Hyperspatial. We have to stay so far away from the star because otherwise, the array won't fold correctly." He raised his head to look through the crystal window at the slightly brighter red star that was the center of the system, the center of his universe. It was bracketed by the mouth of the array. "Something about being able to follow the space-like curves."

"Yes. You're learning quickly. We have to stay away from the gravity well to keep the fold pathway clear of the time-like curves. Long ago, during expansion, we did not fully understand the principle. We could fold, but nothing we sent through ever returned. We thought it a dead end."

"But how did they learn to go so far from the star then?"

"Like all great advances, by accident." The old man gestured, and the image of a woman sprang into the grey circle of the holotank in front of them. Her olive skin was ruddy at the cheek, her midnight-black hair pinned in an elaborate pile. Her image was static, larger than life, and she wore a pitiless expression. Her green eyes matched theirs, but hers sucked the warmth from the room. Despite the transient nature of the hologram, the boy shivered.

"The Empress," the boy whispered.

"Yes," responded the old man, placing his hand on his knees, "the Empress. She who gives us the power of the machines, the gift of her blood in our veins, the charge to keep the schedule and govern the folds. Her immortal self ordered the first array launched. Had the bot package arrived at its destination without issue, we might never have discovered the principle of a successful fold. But the drones that constructed it were damaged in transit and transposed the figures. They built it, not close to the rich inner system but outside the heliopause. It took them a lifetime to loop the generator around the star—one of ours, at least."

The boy nodded, staring at the hologram. The Empress's likeness transfixed him, but he lingered on her eyes. Knowing he had the Eyes of the Empress was one thing, seeing them in his creche mates another. But to see her looking back at him, with his own eyes, made him feel the weight of his responsibility.

"Harbormaster, what will happen to the girl who quickened the other night?"

"Eh? There was a full crop. Which one do you mean?"

"The one who wasn't like us. Who didn't have the Eyes."

The old man placed a hand on the boy's shoulder. "Do not fear for her. She will receive no training. But the array is large and needs much maintenance. They will find a place for her, tending the gardens or keeping up the bots."

The boy nodded. He seemed about to speak again, but he had no time. The harbormaster rose in dismissal before the boy's mouth opened, and he bit back whatever he had been about to say, bowed quickly, and left.

The youth was intelligent and strong, but his fascination with the ungifted was a problem. He would need to be immersed in his training and kept on the course. But the harbormaster was patient. He had many years of service left in him before death, and the boy would serve eventually. If the youth made a misstep along the way, well, there would be another. There was always more grain in the storehouse.

The harbormaster turned to his console and checked the reports from his station. It was time for business, and he could not afford to seem weak. The readouts showed the fold opening, blue light casting his features in sharp relief as the space outside his window lit with vast energies. Finally, the flickering light stabilized into a blue ring. Satisfied that his board was green and all was ready, he replaced the image of the Empress with the harbormaster of Geneline Ollson.

The old man's voice rapped out, commanding respect. "All looks good for stable passage. Are you ready for inspection?" The woman in the hologram nodded, her blue and slate grey uniform in sharp contrast to his gilded robes. They each reached out to tap commands.

Out in space, two waiting flotillas gleamed dully in the low portlights. Their standard design was a counterpoint to the contrasting uniforms of the two genelines. The simple cigar-shaped ships bore not an Obershire crescent or an Ollson wolf but the simple sun of the empire. The inspection teams flitted across the fold boundary between the two flotillas, careful to stay in the center of the glowing blue ring. They swarmed over the ships, quickly inspecting cargo and manifests while the sub-sentient suit AIs queried logs and seals on each piece of cargo. A thorough inspection was critical. The wealth of the empire passed hands here.

Both sides took less than ten minutes to cover all forty vessels, their simplistic design and basic systems allowing rapid inventory. Both harbormasters received the all-clear from their inspection foremen at nearly the same time, and the crews began heading back across the gulf to their home sides. As the inspectors passed, their suits reflected the harshness of harbor lights.

The Obershire Harbormaster idly counted the flecks of light. *One, two, three...* A standard crew was eight inspectors, averaging five ships a minute. The fold ritual allowed for no more, no less. While there had never been an invasion, paranoia ran deep. But now, there were only six glints.

The old man turned to the Ollson hologram. "Better get the rest of your crew across unless they want to live here. When the last ship is through, I'm cutting the generators. We can't afford the energy."

The woman's brows knit. "I've issued the recall. All of our people should be en route. What are you seeing?" Her hands moved out of view of the hologram pickup. "Just a moment. It looks like we are light a couple. I'll ask the foreman."

The Obershire Harbormaster sighed, rolling his wrist to check the golden chronometer that hulked there like an ornate crab. "Well, they had better hurry." The dark bulks of the transport ships had started their slide across the invisible line of demarcation, a sedate and controlled movement somehow still managing to evoke a sense of urgency. The main drives stayed silent, but attitude thrusters stuttered in the darkness, great whales driven by tiny remora.

The Ollson harbormaster pursed her lips. "We're showing four suit malfunctions. They're helping two navigate back across, but the other two are reporting dead thrusters. We have to work on recovery. I need more time."

The Obershire harbormaster turned to look out the window as his hand draped on the control console before him. His fingers were near the section that controlled the fold generators. "The time is the time." His eyes scanned the region of space he had last seen the Ollson team working, his ocular implant tying into station sensors and brightening the dark starfield.

Suddenly, his vision blurred out white. "*What the hell was that?*" Warning klaxons sounded, a cacophony in the small room. As his implants ramped the gain back down, the harbormaster saw the source of the light. Two tiny new suns had bloomed, not far out among the ships where they ought to be, but much closer. Suit-mounted drives, and not the small ones. Assault armor. The old man turned in horror to the Ollson hologram.

"Are you *insane?* You realize what this means?" His hands began to dance across the console, only to find the comm array lifeless. He sucked in a breath and turned back to the Ollson image. "What the fuck is wrong with you people? Executor Obershire won't stand for this! He'll come after you." He paused, his eyebrows raising. "That's what you want. Isn't it? No! There hasn't been a war in a thousand years. Not since the Mendicants and never between genelines. You're insane! Why?" His eyes bulged in panic even as the braking burn of the two incoming suited forms cut off, casting the control room back into darkness.

The Ollson woman smiled. "You are a fool, *helvítis Skoffin.*" she spat, the words as sharp and angular as she, "and I will be glad to see you burn. We have seen you grow fat, secure in your gilded castles on the periphery. You have driven up our costs until we can barely live." What was she talking about? He was the harbormaster. He merely ran the port. Executor Dorian was the head of the geneline. He set the rates!

The woman leaned forward, her face filling the hologram pickup. The harbormaster shrank back at the force of her gaze.

"But no longer, *Brunthró.*"

He began frantically sealing his suit, the glittering brocade of his vestments now flailing like the death throes of a gilded octopus. His green eyes had lost all pride and arrogance, becoming those of a caged animal, desperate. The hologram snapped out. He fumbled in the dark, finally fastening his suit seals. He began to cast about for his helmet, cursing steadily, his hands shaking.

As he moved around the control console, he saw the helmet lying on the ground, knocked there during the fight to get his suit sealed. He stooped to pick it up, stood, and froze, the helmet hanging from his fingertips. He shook his head once, sure his implants were malfunctioning, but the image persisted. On the control room window, two forms crouched in the vacuum, black and dripping malevolence. Two great spiders, mechanical manipulators interspersed with human arms and legs. Their faceless heads stared at him. Then one reared its human hands and arms back. Its head tipped slightly away from the glass as its other limbs held tightly.

The harbormaster started to scream as he realized the thing's intent, but by then, the two great fists had fallen. The window shattered, shotgunning armored glass into space. The other spider reached in and grabbed him by his chest plate, its hand spanning his body. It flipped him out into the pitiless vacuum. His face twisted into a permanent rictus as the scream froze on his lips.

The harbormaster's body continued to orbit the star, silent evidence of the violence of war out in the black. His implants slowly began to spin down, the tiny computers faithfully enhancing and recording images for a brain that no longer held a mind. His personal path around the little red dwarf began to diverge from the harbor array, but as he spun sedately in the frozen dark, his implants recorded the glints and figures of the rest of the harbor crew. Lonely no more, he was joined by many others in their slow dance through the vacuum.

2

IN WHICH THERE IS FENCING

Hear thee, oh reader mine
And heed the tale I tell
Knowledge had he clearly
As he sat upon his high throne

For a blissful moment, the sound of footsteps on the decking was the only noise in the corridor. The last exchange had left Erick on the defensive, not a position to which he was accustomed. As he mulled over Dorian's assertion, his security alerted him to some maintenance bots through the next set of doors, diligently attempting to remove the residue of human occupation.

He paused before triggering the door open and drew up near the corridor window, hoping to preserve this rare moment of privacy. Ever since the Black Guard had pushed the latest system updates, the *Sleipnir's* myriad of support systems and robots seemed less obedient. He frowned. The least the Empress could do was make her spying clandestine.

Dorian must have seen his expression. "What now? Don't look so sour. See how she throws those centurions!" His guffaw echoed, the sound sharp and the echo round in the corridor. "I've no doubt she'll fetch a good bit of dowry for you whenever you finally decide to marry her off!" Erick realized with a start that through the window were the training bays. He forced a smile as he saw his daughter through the glass. She coiled and sprang, dancing between her guards. She had braided her blonde hair tightly to her skull, a style she'd picked up from a trip to Adebe territory some years back. The heavy crash of a soldier in full armor shook the floor under Erick's feet. Bryn had already turned her eyes to those of her personal guard, who remained standing, her breath steady.

The fight wasn't fair and never would be. The exotic matter woven through her bones and muscles made her stronger than any five armored men, and the synthetic neurons that enhanced her reflexes kept her far ahead of any unaugmented human. She had enjoyed fighting from a young age, though, and Erick had encouraged and trained her. Even if she'd likely never need to use her skills, a sharpness of mind came with the sharpness of body.

Erick turned slightly toward Dorian, his green eyes stabbing out from below his short-cropped blond hair. He opaqued the window with a brush of his hand. "My daughter is quite capable of making her own decisions."

Dorian shook his head. The jewels in his red beard swayed and accented the gesture with the sound of beads clacking. "I may never understand your thinking. Crying shame to waste such a beauty." He followed this with what Erick could only assume was meant to be a grunt of admiration.

Erick felt his blood begin to rise as he turned away from the window. He gestured vaguely down the corridor and began to walk, his hand returning to stroke his own neatly trimmed beard. *Time to move on to business.* Before he put their already tenuous alliance in jeopardy with a carefully considered right hook.

This Summit had brought with it unpleasant news. Dorian had just told Erick of the incursions of Revenants on the frontier—not the small raids that were the normal background noise of life on the periphery but more significant. They had almost lost a foundry star, the Revenants' tactics moving from the usual smash and grab to landing boarding parties at the mining rigs. They had killed the security and kept the techs alive to continue to run the collection fields.

As Erick heard Dorian follow him down the corridor, he turned their discussion away from forced marriage. "Have you seen that behavior from the Revenants before? It seems like something must have changed to drive them to this."

Dorian chuffed. "Changed? Hah! We have done the same things as always. Nothing that I can think of might have driven them to try and hold our stations. But I wouldn't worry too much about it. We had set our guard numbers based on what we had seen from them before. We will just have to increase the complement of soldiers and perhaps include some heavier armament. A twenty percent increase in combat capability should be more than sufficient. The Revenants are rabble, after all. Reliance on numbers will only get them so far." He paused to look at Erick sideways. "Of course, this increase in security at the foundry stars will come at a cost…"

Erick sighed inwardly, keeping his smile fixed. Dorian's greed was boringly predictable. "Of course. Security is important, Dorian, but I doubt very much it would increase your production costs *that* much. We will have to negotiate with the genelines downstream to see what they can afford to absorb. Our margins have never been so *fat*." He couldn't resist the gentle emphasis on the last word. Dorian's significant bulk took most of the corridor. *Why doesn't he at least take metabolizers? Is it some twisted vanity?*

Dorian snapped his eyes up to Erick and then grinned, the rubies in his gold-capped teeth glinting a macabre red. "Hah! I knew you had a sense of humor after all. So, it's decided. We'll bring the matter to Summit tomorrow."

Erick nodded, coming to a stop. His ocular showed maintenance bots and a few other people behind the doors they stood beside. "Indeed. The change in the Revenant behavior will affect us. We can decide on specifics tomorrow with the others." Erick selected Dorian's proposal in his ocular and added his Executor's seal to endorse it. He sent it to Dorian, who nodded. Erick cleared his throat. "And now I am afraid I must take my leave. Until tomorrow." He bowed slightly to Dorian, the barest inclination of the head.

Dorian nodded. "Good, good. I look forward to tomorrow then. And tell that daughter of yours I'm happy to introduce her to any of my sons!" His laughter echoed off the corridor as he left. Erick watched him go until the door swung shut. *I doubt very much that any of your sons would come away unscathed from meeting my daughter, you insolent inbred rassgat.* He had no way of knowing for sure, but it was very suspicious that no one had seen an Obershire daughter in many years. Yes, cloning was the only way to ensure the geneline wasn't diluted, but culling out the females was barbaric.

Erick stood in the corridor and breathed deeply, his thoughts turning toward Summit. Negotiations were usually straightforward, with each geneline bringing their revised estimates to the table. From there, it was a simple game of mathematics to settle exchange rates, times, and quantities of goods. All Executors were bound to their agreement under threat of excommunication. This had kept the peace since the formation of the empire. The Empress had little room for mercy. Dorian's move to renegotiate trade rates between his geneline and Erick's would affect the entire supply chain, all the way up to the Black Throne.

Erick needed some advice, and none knew more than the dead.

3

IN WHICH THE DEAD ARE WOKEN, SORT OF

Hear thee, oh reader mine
And heed the tale I tell
But knowledge can no wisdom
Bring without the mirror to show

Erick was old. He felt it in his bones, despite their solidity. He felt it in the slide of tendon under his skin, felt the age behind his eyes. He carried it in his unchanging body—each moment stored away like a tiny straw added to his back. Solid and broad though he was, and upright though he walked, he could feel the weight of ages. In times like this, he sought the comfort of others, far elder. Nothing quite like the company of the dead to make you feel young again.

The crypt was ancient, older than Erick, than his mother, than his grandfather. The ancients had built it after the Founding Wars. Each generation had modified it until it had reached the best possible design. Well, the best that imperial technology had to offer. The Empress had not yet outlawed the practice, but the Mendicant Wars had made it clear that her benevolence had limits. The fear of machine and mind together was solid deterrence against those who sought to entomb themselves in metal minds and join her in immortality.

Whenever he left the home system, he always visited the crypt. There, his ancestors lay entombed, quantum bits and entangled bytes trapping their consciousness in an undying web. Someday he would join them, would go to the download chamber at the center and give himself, body and mind, to the future of his geneline. The first few times he woke, he might even remember himself.

When he traveled, he took the recordings of those who might offer counsel with him. His mother always told him it was foolish to take such treasures from their redoubt. Erick saw no point in resources unused. Was he to be a hermit, shut up forever in the home system while the dead whispered in his ear? He'd rather they whisper when he needed them most.

He stood now in the chamber at the heart of the *Sleipnir*, inside layer after layer of decking and armor. No need to take too much risk, after all. It was not a large room, barely enough to pace in thought. Along one steel-grey wall stood three glowing cubes, suspended by fields. Physical wires snaked from them like protein spikes from a virus, grossly elongated to plunge into a nest of cables that disappeared into the wall behind them. Interfacing directly with quantum storage devices required a delicate balance. Each time the data was observed, it collapsed just slightly differently with a little more degradation. But that was worth it now. Dorian's claims were likely false, but Erick needed to know more about the Revenants. If they were growing more aggressive, they might someday grow worthy of attention. It had been a long time since Ollson forces had engaged in full combat operations, and there was no reason he couldn't set a few traps of his own. If Revenants wanted to seize imperial assets, Erick might have a good training opportunity for his forces. Perhaps this wasn't all bad.

In his ocular, Erick called a ghost. They did not always answer the dead. Sometimes they couldn't make the connection, couldn't coalesce back into the standing wave pattern of a mind, or what was left of one.

The far-left cube hummed and pulsed, its surface twisting like an insane oil slick. Watching it hurt his mind, dimensionality abandoned in a gyre of colors with no name. Shortly, his ocular painted a face in midair before him.

"Siggurd. It is good to see you, ancestor."

The face was long and hard, beard short and sharp. The edges faded and blurred as the mind behind it fought to recall itself. Image was a part of self, and often the first aspect of personality to be lost. Some only spoke. This face could do both.

"Young Erick." His voice blurred into digital static at the low register. "You have woken me yet again. What makes you worthy of this much of my counsel?"

Humility was clearly not a trait the old generations valued. "Honored ancestor, it has been a hundred and seventy-two years since we spoke last. I do not seek your counsel lightly. The Revenants have returned."

The face appeared to expend great effort to look shocked. "Revenants? Nonsense. They were routed out and destroyed before my time, at the end of the Mendicant Wars. My father swept them from our systems before I was quickened. There can be no Revenants. It is a trick, a deception. Have you seen them?"

Erick shook his head, clasping his hands behind his back. "No, ancestor, not with my own eyes. Or even in Ollson space. But they have been raiding along the periphery for a hundred years, off and on. Their return was noted but not particularly relevant. They were easily repelled."

"Then why have you awakened me, young Erick? It sounds as if they are no great threat to the glory of the empire."

"That much I believe to be true. But Dorian of Obershire claims they attempted to take one of his mining stations. He's going to provide his evidence at Summit tomorrow."

The face laughed and then froze, looping back to calm and then back to laughter. A demon's cackle filled the air. "Obershire! They lack all honor. They are obsessed with money. Never trust those who pray to Gullveig. Wealth is not power. Power is power. Dorian's words mean nothing."

Gullveig. Vanir gods. Siggurd really is laying it on a bit thick. But Erick paused, troubled. Siggurd's words rang true enough, close enough to his own thinking. But something still nagged at him. His ancestor thought the Revenants had been thoroughly destroyed. After they had tried to take advantage of the Empress's weakness following the Mendicant Wars, the Hundred Genelines had been given very specific instructions. Give no quarter. The uprising had been over almost before it began.

Erick steepled his hands under his chin as he turned to walk as much as the small room would allow. "Honored Siggurd, tell me, where did the Revenants come from?"

The eyebrows on the floating face raised as Siggurd attempted to show emotion. "Fruits of the poisoned tree. The humans that were tainted, sullied by the Mendicants. The foul machines enslaved humans, made them do their bidding, bound them in mind and soul. Death was mercy for them."

Erick nodded. *Nothing new there.* "Yes, I know the histories. Thank you, ancestor." He began to move his hand in the pattern that would send the face back to its cube and the sleep of the dead.

The voice boomed out. "Manners, boy! You have awakened me! I will not be denied my due again!"

Erick grimaced. Confined without a body, a mind existing with no stimulation, the inhabitants of the glowing cubes craved input. The mere sense of self, limbs, and knowing where they were, let alone the input of real eyes and mouth and nose. It was tradition for the living to offer their senses to the dead on occasion.

"What do you request, Siggurd?"

"Honey rolls. Saffron. And mead. We will blot the gods before I sleep."

Ah yes, the gods. Each time it seemed Siggurd became more and more devout in his afterlife. But who could be sure if the gods existed on this side of the veil? Best not to tempt fate. At worst, it cost him a little time. Giving Siggurd the feed of his senses did a lot to keep the old man somewhat sane. A ghost could not taste the rolls and mead alone.

Throughout the ceremony, Erick's mind wandered. He said the words and felt Siggurd savor the taste of the honey and saffron. The Revenants were supposed to have fallen from the galaxy. Their lives snuffed out in the same righteous fury that destroyed the Mendicants. But they had returned, subhuman at first, their raids marked by savagery and blood. Now, though, they showed the beginning of strategy if Dorian's words were true. That was troubling, and it warranted diving farther back.

As he spoke the words for blot to the elder gods with the zealous Siggurd, he stewed, impatient to finish the ritual and move on. Finally, they hailed the last of the gods, and he motioned Siggurd back into not-being. Erick would speak with one more, the oldest ancestor in the crypt who still responded to a summons. He had brought her in the hopes she would not be needed.

Now, to some answers. As he summoned her, the center cube swirled. Then, it dimmed and slowed. Erick frowned, his brows furrowed. He waited. After what seemed like an eternity, the cube finally moved again but slowly. There was no face this time, no grand visage of the ancient one. Only a voice, digital wind in the trees, the banshee's whisper caressing him through the link.

"*Flón*. You still serve."

"Honored ancestor. Aslog. I greet you." The old formal words sounded stiff on his tongue, iron and salt.

Her reply was long in coming. "Never has the great tree sallowed as now. Never has the Line fallen so low, foolish boy!"

Well. Good. She at least had not gotten worse. "I beseech you, tell me what you know of the old ones who fell to slavery and fared beyond the empire."

A horrible keening laughter filled his ears, grating on his nerves. His jaw clamped tightly against the onslaught. "The ravens know all! They know all. They fly over the nine realms, aye, and bring him all the wisdom and goings-on of the world. Would that they were yours, foolish boy!"

This was getting nowhere. He hoped she wasn't beyond reach. The storage cube made him think this might be her last foray into the land of the living. He needed a new tack. "Tell me, where are the ravens now?"

"Ravens, dark and dismal of soul. Aye, you might seek them out, were you a better man. You might bring them to him, the long-spear, the one-who-walks, bring them to him, and they will tell the story. But not I! Those that were cast out are gone for a reason. And that story is better left untold." The voice rose in a keening, wordless moan; a crashing wave of sound that dissolved into digital chaos. He cut the feed.

Ravens. Long spear. She had finally gone mad. Erick sighed as he checked the three cubes automatically, ensuring telemetry and reading from each were within limits. Siggurd had seemed sure in his assessment, and Aslog spoke in too many riddles and metaphors. The story she had been about to tell him was with her in whatever afterlife she had found. He needed time and space. And to get away from the undead tomb in the steel heart of the ship. Yes, space to think and to be surrounded by life.

4

IN WHICH THERE ARE MACHINATIONS

―

Power had he, and all he saw
Did bow down to him in worship
And oft did he visit, the green field
Of Ida, and there thought deep and long

Something about the fierce contrast of green life and the stark metal decking invigorated Erick in a way he couldn't explain. As his steps turned toward the center of the ship, he could almost smell the sharp pine and soft flowers, the pungent smell of tomato vines that awaited him.

It took him back to learning to work the garden as a child, gently placing tomato cuttings into their holders in the nutrient bath as the fish glinted and flashed below. As Executor, his mother had been busy, but she'd always taken the time to join him in the gardens during his lifecycle lessons. Life on a ship revolved around birth and death, growth and decay. While he knew he'd never be the one tending it, his tutors had deemed it critical for him to build an appreciation of the world around him. He didn't need much coercion when he was young. The tomatoes plucked from the vine were always better before the chefs had touched them.

As he grew older, his studies became more rigorous. His tutors would always know where to look when he was not present for his lesson on higher mathematics or field theory. Now, Erick walked, hands clasped behind his back and lost in thought until the light of the fusion tunnel above him drew him out of his reverie. His feet had taken him to the gardens. He inhaled deeply, taking in the smell of the greenery around him and closing his eyes to absorb the fierce light of the artificial sun.

His face warmed, and he stood for a moment, feeling the gentle hum of the decking under his feet. He opened his eyes, and a flash of motion caught his eye, a massive butterfly floating by. Its bulbous thorax and iridescent wings seemed to hang suspended for an instant, and then it fluttered hard and climbed away. While animals needed higher gravity for bone density and muscle mass, the geneticists had long ago optimized the garden ecosystem for the inner deck's gentle quarter gravity. The fantastic insects were a testament to their skill. He couldn't help but appreciate that the geneticists had taken a little creative license with some of the species. He watched the neon blue butterfly land on one of the whisker pines. It gently flexed its wings in a dazzling display of color.

He began to walk along the garden path that led to the farm squares. As he did, a notice flashed in his ocular that Bryn would join him there in a few minutes. He grinned as he sent her a read receipt. He was easy enough to predict when it came to the garden, even now. Erick followed the path through the whisker pine grove. Bryn would be at Summit tomorrow, and he was curious to know her thoughts on how she might handle the situation with the Geneline Obershire.

The Ollsons had good relations with the Genelines Smith and McGinnis, both heavy equipment manufacturers. They could count others as allies as well. Amari Adebe and Zehra Osman were both next-level customers, trading directly with the Ollsons. They would likely join Erick in ensuring that the Obershire increase of twenty percent in guards didn't translate into a twenty percent increase in cost. With a coalition of voices, they might even get close to finding out the actual cost of the increase. Erick was sure Dorian had padded his estimate. The only question was by how much.

The path wound downhill toward the center of the garden, and Erick enjoyed the lightness of each step. *I should come here more.* The thought rose unbidden, tearing him away from his musings. He rounded the last corner before the farm squares, and they spread out before him, each long block of hydroponic bed like the squares on a chessboard. Tall climbing tomato hung from vine supports that rimmed the thick mats of leafy greens. Beneath them, through the translucent sides of the nutrient bath, flashing silver scales revealed schools of fish. Bryn was sitting on a low bench across from a field of hydroponic cabbage. Her head moved sedately as she watched the waves of bobbing plants, her plaits now twisted into buns. Schools of fish darted below the surface and sent ripples dancing across the floating green balls of cabbage. He walked over in her direction, and as he drew near, he called out. "Hungry?"

She turned back over her shoulder to look at him, eyes squinting against the glare. "Hah. Not that hungry. I prefer my food prekilled. Besides, it doesn't look like you brought a rod, old man."

He attempted a stern look, failing miserably. "Now listen here. That's no way to talk to someone who's only a few centuries your senior. Look, not a grey hair on my head!"

She laughed, and he returned her smile. "That's because there's getting to be *no* hair on your head, with every cut a little shorter. Eventually, you'll have it shaved, but that won't change the color, will it? Can't be missing the details, after all. I need you at peak for Summit."

He sat next to her on the bench, stretching one arm out along the back. He crossed one leg and tapped the heel of his boot with the other as he began speaking. "Look at you, all business all the time. When did you get to be so focused?"

She shifted to face him, brushing a strand of hair from her line of sight. "When I noticed you ambling off toward the gardens after a brief conversation with that insufferable twat Dorian."

He frowned at her. "Language, please, my delicate constitution. He is a twat, though. And I'm going to have to be more careful. If you knew something was up that easily, who knows who else might."

She tapped his knee as she said, "Not to worry, Father dearest, only I know of your deep and abiding love for growing things. I and the rest of the garden staff who constantly have to herd the agri-bots out of your way as you wander misty-eyed through hill and mechanical dale."

He grimaced. "Right. Well, first, point taken. Second, I did want to ask you your thoughts on tomorrow." He raised a hand and twisted his wrist slightly, fingers open. The air around them became wavy, distorting the view of the garden. Bryn raised one eyebrow at him.

"Really? Seems a bit cloak and dagger of you. We are on our own ship after all."

He smiled back. "Yes, well, ever since the latest update, the bots haven't been exactly mindful of my privacy orders. Besides, I carry this gizmo around everywhere. Be a shame not to use it." He pulled a tiny brown bead from the hem of his jacket, and it pulsed with a gentle inner amber light. The field around them strengthened to the point where only a vague and formless world existed outside.

"Well, that should do it. We have about fifteen minutes until the field dissipates. So here's what I learned during my short chat with your beloved cousin Dorian." She made a face at the mention of his name. "The Revenants are getting more aggressive." He paused to see her reaction.

As he expected, it was minimal. "So? They raid and take a bit more on the edges. It's not like they are going to be able to make an appreciable dent in our input materials." She wasn't wrong, technically. Geneline storehouses were essentially impermeable.

"They will if there's nothing in the storehouse." She raised an eyebrow. "They tried to take and hold a foundry star. Did a pretty decent job of it, too. Kept it running, at least. Obershire had to decant some shock troopers to deal with it."

She raised both eyebrows at this. "That's new. They raid. They run. They can't use our tech, and they had to know there would be a response. Anything else?"

He shook his head. "No, that's the sum of it. Dorian says he is going to have to up his guard presence by twenty percent."

She moved her hand to her chin, and he could see the wheels turning. "Well, that little shit. No way he's that casual about a twenty percent manning increase. I bet it's not even half that. Did he show you the proof?"

"No, but he's going to bring it up at Summit tomorrow. So I'm assuming it isn't a complete fabrication, though I wouldn't put it past him."

Bryn nodded. "No, he's not suicidal. This seems more than just increasing costs and calling it good. *Drullusokkar.*"

The edge of Erick's mouth twitched up toward a smile. "No, no, it's much more important than an increase in trade rates, though you're right. We'll keep that as low as we can. I'm much more interested in why the Revenants have shifted tactics. I doubt they just wanted to take a foundry star because they thought it would be a neat project. They may be basic and brutish, but they're not dumb." Her head bobbed in agreement. Erick paused, pensive. "What do you think their objective was if they knew they would lose the star eventually?"

Her response came immediately. "Clearly, they were looking to see what the response was."

He smiled and nodded. "I think you're right. And I think they aren't done yet either. One star, one data point, but they need to see what dearly beloved Dorian will do."

Bryn furrowed her brow and looked slightly down. "But what's the point? I mean, they take a star. Obershires take it back. Even if they find out what the response is, they don't have the resources or tech to take and hold anything of value."

Erick leaned forward, and the bead began to pulse red. He put it back to the hem of his jacket, and it stuck, indistinguishable from the others. "Yes, kiddo, that's the real question. Why indeed? It looks like our time is almost up. I want you there for Summit tomorrow sitting with our delegation." Her eyes grew a little wide. "Don't worry. I'm not going to ask you to say anything official. I want you to listen, though, to the room and the people. *Really* observe. I have an inkling that this Revenant incursion isn't the only one that's happened on a periphery system, nor will it be the last."

■■■

By the time Erick made it back to the lower decks and his stateroom, the lights had already started to dim. He tossed his jacket toward the servitor in the corner as he walked through the doors, the robot diligently catching the garment and gliding off toward the closet space. Time to do a little planning. He had an agent in the Geneline Cavanaugh who was usually reliable. He knew his geneline had allies willing to help with the negotiations but needed to know who else on the periphery had run into the Revenants recently. He packaged a query on Revenant activity into a physical message tape, encrypting it with a dummy genome to which he knew the source had access.

He'd rather have used the genome of the source themselves for proper security. However, the source was careful, and he didn't know who it was. *Probably better not to have it pointing directly at the recipient either.* The film, a barely present gossamer of carbon with the encrypted message stamped into it atom by atom, went into the transfer case at his desk and was then fired directly to the fold array. The schedule showed the next fold to Cavanaugh space in an hour, the return not until late into his night. He'd check for the reply in the morning but was not hopeful it would be back in time for Summit.

In the meantime, he sent a few open channel messages via the local network to the other genelines, inquiring about any activity on the periphery. He didn't think he'd get anything from them in the open. Survival depended on cooperation, but that didn't mean they had a complete absence of competition. Knowledge was the only real power.

Finally, Erick retired to bed and clarified the window, the light of the other ships stitching neat rows of inky-black windows across the scattered starfield. A few of them, illuminated by vanity lights, painted fantastic images against the stars. Tomorrow would come soon enough, and he could use the rest. Without some distraction, he knew his mind would continue to grind away, so he leaned back and closed his eyes. He scrolled through his personal music list, the new and the old side by side. After going through the more recent works, he settled on the ancient form of opera, one of only a few that had made it through the wars. He let the soaring notes envelop him. Sometimes, older really was better.

5

IN WHICH AN UNEVENTFUL BREAKFAST HAPPENS

> *Wisdom he sought, but ne'er found*
> *Not in the heights of song*
> *Or the comfort of lovers*
> *Nor ever in his own mind-halls*

Erick awoke with a nearly audible snap, mentally running through the checklist for the morning as he rose. By the time he made it to the mirror, the fields had dressed him, his usual clothing joining him in a marionette dance before seamlessly sliding onto him and joining together. He inspected the handiwork, ensuring the fields had smoothed each hair in his beard into place. Some genelines took Summit as a chance to show off, and he had no doubt the other Executors would talk about his relatively sparse and martial look in low tones over a wide array of amuse-bouches. No matter. The Ollson name was always associated with a conservative outlook in deed and word.

As he looked in the mirror, Erick remembered the only time his mother had bowed to fashion. It was Summit that Bryn was born and the last before Erick had formally assumed the Executorship. His mother had set her personal field to suspend tiny castoffs from the carbon trade into delicate constellations that mirrored the sky on Karvasok the night her granddaughter was born to the Ollson surrogates. The diamond constellations followed her every move. While the other genelines merely saw the normally stiff-necked Ollsons attempting to bow to convention, every Ollson subject on Karvasok who saw her sitting at the assembly table knew those stars like the back of their hand. It was a singularly uplifting gesture, marking something powerful only to the Ollsons. She never mentioned the patterns to the other dignitaries, and they never asked. It was enough that Erick knew.

He shook himself from the reverie. His morning briefing scrolled past on his implant. He'd missed a good part of it and started it over as he left his rooms. His eyes flicked across the usual reports of movement of goods, operating capacities at Ollson factory worlds, vault status, charge cycles and timelines for the various transit stars across his space. His feet carried him toward the galley, and he pulled himself away from the manifest listing of the latest inter-geneline transfers at the smell of fresh-baked goods. He followed his nose, the smell drawing him toward the main dining room. Bryn, of course, was already there, stirring a spoon idly in her cup of coffee as her eyes jittered back and forth. No doubt on her ocular, reading the same reports as he.

"Good morning, daughter mine. Anything jump out at you from the morning brief?" He slid a chair out across from her and sat, crossing an ankle across his knee. The smell of something, earth and spice and a little bit sharp, intensified as the door to the kitchens opened. He was under no illusion as to the nature of the food on a spacecraft, but the staff still managed to pull off a pretty good approximation of home.

Karvasok orbited a fantastic G-type main series, as close as the ancestors could find to the throne world in Ollson territory. One of the many things that grew well was grain, and as the server bots brought out steaming cakes and rolls, Erick appreciated that the staff had brought enough flour to last the trip. It beat the hardtack bars that served as food for more austere journeys. Erick flipped a napkin out of its ornate ring and set it across his leg. "Bryn," he spoke again gently, "anything interesting?"

She tossed her head, clearing her hair back, and he saw her eyes focus on him. "Just the usual boring nonsense about shipping and production. Looks like everything is… normal." A slightly furrowed brow punctuated her pause. "Did you see the Obershire transfer, though? Connection stayed open an extra three minutes. Something about a suit malfunction in one of the inspection teams."

Erick grunted by way of acknowledgment. "I did notice that. Means we'll have to adjust cost, at the very least. Wasn't enough to impact charging for the next connection, though." He sighed dramatically. "You'd think by now we'd have a decent harbormaster at that post. After the last one missed the timing, the message should be quite clear."

The previous harbormaster cost them an entire cycle's profit with his sloppy execution and lack of diligence. As Executor, Erick usually tried to lean toward the love of his people as much as he could, but it wasn't the only thing that power demanded. His mother had always taught him that fear and love were both necessary for a ruler, and in this case, he could not afford to spare the rod. The factories had to work.

They had to trade their goods to the neighboring genelines, and so on. All the wealth and riches magnified as they flowed to the throne world, but flow they must, for the empire of humanity to function. Stability and peace demanded that all keep to the schedule and do their part.

So Erick had taken the harbormaster, who had missed the timing of a transfer, to observe the factories on Karvasok from orbit. He showed the man all the billions of people who relied on them to live. He had explained to him, as gently as he could but clearly, the critical role of the trade in their society. It was the hardest thing Erick had done to keep his face calm and neutral as he explained this to him and to all the Ollson worlds who watched the feed. And then he'd put the harbormaster out the airlock.

Bryn nodded at his mention of the last harbormaster, her mouth moving to a sardonic smile. "You really just can't get good help these days. I do hope this one doesn't get herself into a cold orbit as well. The good news is that it looks like the transfer was complete. All the logs are accounted for and so on. If only Summit issues would resolve themselves in such a mundane fashion."

Erick nodded in agreement and gestured to a serving bot. It trundled forward with a plate of scones, and he selected one at random. "You've had some time to sleep on it. What do you think we should do today to address Dorian?"

Bryn began buttering her kveik roll, the slightly spicy citrus scent wafting over to him. "Well, we know what's coming from dear old Dorian, so we probably ought to speak to Francis about what to expect. Lanaria and Zehra as well—they're not that far removed from the foundries. They'll care about the impact to shipping too."

He nodded in agreement and bit into the scone, the tart sweetness of blueberry flavoring his thoughts as he chewed deliberately. He wanted to see where she would go with this. After a few moments of silence, he nodded to her. "And?"

She set her roll down and leaned back in her chair, a slight curl grazing the corner of her mouth. "Father dearest, are you testing me?"

"Not at all, daughter mine. I want to know what you think we should do. A true leader weighs all counsel before making a decision."

She laughed at him. "As if anything I say would change your mind in the slightest."

He made a mockingly injured face, hand to his heart. "My dear, you wound me! I always listen to you. You are, after all, my favorite daughter."

"I'm your only daughter, you senile old man, or had you forgotten? No, of course not." She waved her hand in dismissal. "Here, we'll first contact Zehra. Always an excuse for you two to get together. She's probably got the most to lose as the Osmans buy the bulk of our second-level production. All the heavy isotopes, most of the polymers, pretty much all of our nanofibers and carbon lattice. So we point out that if she doesn't want a significant impact to her heavy manufacturing customers, she should work with us to corner dear Dorian early in the negotiations." He nodded to her encouragingly. "Then, Francis and Lanaria will likely fall in line behind us. They're farther downstream as far as production goes, but they still need a lot of our complex biochemicals and volatiles for their processes. All of that's going to be affected if Dorian tries to hike his bottom line up, so he's already facing resistance. And… he'll know that. Shit."

Erick was laughing now, his straight face coming slightly unglued at the edges. "Don't worry. You're right. We need to do all those things. Zehra sends her regards, by the way."

Bryn picked up her knife and pointed it at him. "I wondered why you seemed so calm this morning. Already made all the appropriate noises, have we?" She dipped the knife back into the butter, the blade flashing as she made the slashing motion in mock anger.

Erick grinned. "Yes, yes, it's all taken care of. I knew something was up when Dorian broke the news to me in the hallway. He'd already been making noises about the Revenants raiding his stars in the correspondence leading up to Summit. Might as well have broadcast his intent on all channels."

She nodded appreciatively. "It's a good thing you're not going anywhere soon; I'm still learning to be as pessimistic and paranoid as I'll need to be to take up the reins here."

Erick nodded back at her. "Don't worry, daughter. Another fifty years or so and you'll have me looking like a naïve saint. I'm sure of it."

6

IN WHICH PLANS ARE LAID

Enemies sought him, and he they
Jealous they were
And guarded their treasure
In hope of keeping their own value

After breakfast, father and daughter walked toward the lift shaft on the outside of their flagship. They sat in comfortable silence, feeling their limbs grow heavier as the lift took them forward. Erick let his mind run idle, staring out the transparent bubble as the ship raced by just overhead. The eight great drive spines arced back behind the ship, trailing like the tentacles of some mythic sea creature. As the transport rounded the curve of the foredecks, the drive spines dropped back out of view, and he turned his eyes forward.

Weight slowly disappeared again as the path of the lift took them closer to the spin axis. Erick hooked the toe of one foot under the floor bar as he felt the deceleration. The forward observation deck and shuttle docking loomed into view. Down no longer being a concept with any meaning, his mind flipped the scene, and suddenly they drifted upside down in a bubble of air atop a leviathan. A gentle chime sounded, and the doors opened.

He pushed off and dove down into the vast, sweeping hallway. The crew moved with the easy grace of those long accustomed to microgravity. Bryn followed along at a respectful distance, and he gently tapped the wall as he approached the end of the corridor to slow himself. He twisted and turned, the motion aligning his feet toward the approaching bulkhead. He landed, shoes gripping the wall gently with just enough electrostatic tension to keep him from rebounding away.

Bryn landed beside him, her feet as light as his. Erick gestured down the hallway toward the waiting shuttles, and she nodded, kicking back off the bulkhead as she drifted through the corridor. She reached out a hand toward one door ahead of her, and the opening glowed green as it recognized her. He followed her in, and their light exosuits floated from the storage locker, the ship's fields affixing them before they had made it to their crash couches. The straps rose and fell around them on the shuttle fields, fixing them firmly into the tiny craft.

A much more primitive design than the larger *Sleipnir*, the shuttle had a miniature fusion reactor buried under the base of the forward nose cone that supplied both power and propulsion, with small attitude jets embedded in the outer skin. It looked small and inconspicuous but was far overbuilt for a craft its size. Some of the other genelines would opt for more opulent transportation, but the shuttle was supposed to be utilitarian, and it was effective. It would be the fastest thing around, at least. He checked those systems now as they brought the reactor online, Bryn's voice murmuring checklist items as he answered her in short monosyllables. While routine, space travel was anything but safe. Erick had no desire to test out the survival units built into their seats.

While Bryn finished her checklist, Erick keyed a comm channel. "*Sleipnir* control, Viking Zero-One will be departing as fragged. Say status of Zero-Two." Erick didn't like traveling with a large entourage, but his security chief had insisted on his support staff at least getting there before him.

The response came in clipped, no-nonsense from the on-watch deck officer. "Viking Zero-One, you're approved for departure, your discretion. Viking Zero-Two landed one-five mics ago and reports all clear."

"Roger that, *Sleipnir* Control, departure at my discretion."

Bryn finished her final few steps, and he nodded in satisfaction. She gestured to him for the controls, but he shook his head, raising his hands behind his head and interlacing his fingers. "All yours, just go easy on the juice until we're clear of the main bay."

She snorted and grinned at him. "Yes, Father." Her hands tapped the glowing icons in front of her, and they sprang off the panel, enveloping her hands in sharp blue and orange. She gestured precisely, attitude thrusters sending ringing reverberations through the hull of the little craft as she blipped them.

Bryn nodded her chin up once as the vessel moved away from the docking ring, grunting with satisfaction as the collision warnings moved from yellow to green and finally disappeared. Erick feigned relaxation and a disinterested expression, but his eyes danced across the instruments. False-color radiation patterns overlayed radar returns. The small glowing cursors marking other ships created a riot of color across his vision. His personal view in his ocular faded slightly to emphasize Bryn and his shared data environment. The shuttle's flight path marker danced and spun as Bryn aligned them toward the large Summit ship, approaching vector green but with an alarming trend to yellow as she lined up.

He glanced sidelong at her. "Cutting it a touch close. Aren't we?" His voice was gentle but firm. He had complete confidence that the automatic traffic control system wouldn't allow an unsafe input, but that didn't necessitate blind trust. *Trust, but verify.*

Bryn's eyes focused on lining up the flight path marker and killing their slight rotation. "Vector is nominal for the approach, and there's no other traffic in our sector. Worst case, we overshoot a bit, but we are good on fuel for at least ten attempts."

Erick opened his mouth to speak again and then shut it and shrugged noncommittally. "Nothing unsafe, just not how I would do it. Confirm clear?"

"Clear." Bryn twisted her left hand and curled her fingers toward her. He heard the thrumming of the mag fields on the reactor containment step up in volume. "Set full-aspect." Her voice was steady, and he replied by moving his hand across the shared controls that glowed above the panel. The inside bulkheads and seats of the shuttle faded away, replaced by a perfect view of the outside. Erick and Bryn seemed to hang suspended in the vacuum, the full beauty of the other capital ships of the hundred genelines spread around them like a handful of diamonds frozen midthrow.

"Set," he replied. With the other ships surrounding their flight path so closely and the shuttle visuals set to full-aspect, this was going to be an intense trip. He couldn't keep himself from adding, "Ah. Now I see why we are skirting the proximity regulations."

She grinned, not looking away from the shuttle flight path marker as her hands and feet moved to keep the shuttle aligned between the two larger craft. "Standby for burn." He heard a little bit of the Ollson wolf in her. "This is the fun part, after all."

He chuckled and looked aft down the center of the shuttle, revealed in his ocular as a tracing overlay. *Always clear your drive trail.* "Cleared burn on your mark." Bryn moved her left hand forward, rather suddenly in Erick's opinion, and the shuttle snapped forward. The aft view darkened as the shuttle's cameras dropped gain from the intense plume of fusion plasma that now leaped from the rear of the little shuttle. The *Sleipnir* dropped away from them like a rock dropped in a gravity well, rapidly shrinking to just another glowing icon.

They flew the majority of the transfer in silence, absorbed in monitoring the traffic collision avoidance and the ship's internal systems. It seemed they were ahead of the crowd only by a few minutes, as the space around the Summit vessel quickly became crowded with false-color approach vectors. Bryn slowed them early to keep from having to brake hard on arrival. The shuttle could endure over a hundred gravities, but only if the inertial compensators kicked in, and they were energy hungry. Best to keep as much fuel as possible in case of an emergency.

As their shuttle drew closer to the Summit ship, they joined the conga line of craft matching vectors with the bay. Most genelines, he noticed, had not failed to deliver their promise of opulence. Gilded craft hung in various states of relative velocity, swooping on tangent arcs to join the procession lines leading into the gaping maw of the shuttle bay.

The docking system was ready, and Bryn gave it control. Their craft settled into the slightly unnerving solidity of purely automatic systems.

Erick had taught Bryn to fly decades ago, primarily out of a sense of nostalgia from when his mother had taught him how to control the bucking power of a spacecraft. The slightest touch was enough to send this craft leaping nimbly about. Powerful engines and thrusters combined with the lack of atmospheric drag meant truly ferocious velocities were easily achievable—and wickedly fun.

Erick turned his crash couch to face hers as they observed the slowly growing side of their host ship. "Well, I honestly don't have anything for your flying."

Bryn smirked back at him, waiting. "…but?" she said, one eyebrow rising.

"But, oh daughter mine, your decision to choose such an aggressive approach vector was probably not in the best interest of safety. Our departure from the *Sleipnir* would have been just as exciting had you aimed off just a bit more."

She sighed dramatically, moving the back of her hand to her forehead in feigned delicacy. "My goodness, you're right. Whatever was I thinking?" Her arms crossed, and she hooked one ankle over the other, gently floating up against the seat restraints with the motion. "You worry too much. The systems wouldn't have let me lay in the course if it was a problem, and I was trying to beat the rush." She gestured at the hanging baubles of surrounding craft with a sweeping motion. "But clearly, so was everyone else. Besides, don't we have more important things to talk about?"

He sighed inwardly and allowed the diversion. "Yes, but honestly, we can't move forward until tomorrow. As you recall, I've already reached out where appropriate, so once the Obershires formally express their position, we can go from there."

"You mean once Dorian shoots his mouth off. But isn't it worth sending at least a greeting and inquiry to our allies? Perhaps the Osmans? I'd like to know when they plan on being here if they're not already joining us in the queue."

Erick studied the casual furrow of her brow and the flare of her nose as she spoke, the slight shift in her posture. "If you're that interested in Azita's whereabouts, why not simply ask?"

She reached out to slap his knee gently. "Stop! You know I am focused on business, now of all times." Her slight blush gave her away. "Besides, I haven't spoken to Azita Osman in ages. Maybe even since last Summit. I don't really recall."

He grinned at her and chuckled. "Right, right, of course. Silly of me to bring it up."

She turned back to the front of the shuttle. "Yes. Silly. But speaking of the Osmans, I'm assuming you and Zehra have already made dinner plans?"

Erick, to his satisfaction, did not blush. "You know Zehra Osman and I have had a long and fruitful professional relationship. She's one of our oldest allies, after all."

"A professionally horizontal relationship."

"So? Adults can keep business and pleasure separate without having to forego either. A skill you should brush up on, actually."

"Was that an endorsement to begin my own diplomatic liaison?"

"Yes, let's go with that as the word. Diplomatic liaison."

"Right."

They returned to discussing the upcoming meeting as the shuttle's autopilot guided them. Eventually, they grew quiet as the shuttle entered the docking perimeter. Erick's skin tingled as they passed through the field that held a thin atmosphere in the docking bay. The shuttle's display highlighted their berth, between a craft that looked like some deep-sea fish dipped in gold and a rather ornate bronze number covered in what appeared to be human figures lustily engaged in a sumptuous bacchanalia. The landing deck appeared to be above them now, and as they approached, the shuttle rotated. As far as the eye could see, craft lined up, the bay fading to blackness after a few kilometers. The pulsing river of guide lights snaked back, painting a technicolor sky of neon stars on one side of the ring. Back toward the opening, they could just make out the true blackness of space and the dusting of real stars beyond. A gentle thump ran through the shuttle as the landing gear engaged.

Erick began the reactor shutdown sequence. Finally, they had neared the end of the checklist, and Bryn paused to look at him questioningly. "How paranoid are you this time?"

He grinned at her. "Let's leave it primed. Shall we? Plenty of fuel after all, and we won't be here more than a few days." She nodded in agreement, bringing the reactor down shy of fusion temperatures but leaving the shore power engaged and the core preheated. Their light suits enveloped them, the green around the open helmet seal a reassuring sign of atmosphere.

The soft *thunk* of footsteps were the only audible sounds as they walked to the shuttle's door and down to the deck. Erick's eyes wandered the bay. *Who thought that was a good idea?* A particularly ostentatious number a quarter of the way up the ring appeared to be solid diamond. It refracted docking lights across the bay, painting everything in rainbow smears.

Erick breathed the hangar air deeply. It smelled sharp, ozone of high-energy discharge and the burnt metal-on-vacuum. The shuttle popped and tinged gently behind him as the temperature equalized, and he looked over at Bryn. She smiled back and gestured at him to lead the way with a slight bow and gentle cheeky grin. He grunted and pretended not to notice, taking a long stride out ahead. She fell into step just behind and left of him. He clasped his hands behind his back and squared his shoulders as he walked.

In his ocular, Erick reviewed the checklist of items for Summit. His feet followed the blue line in his vision that would lead him to the conference. He rehearsed a little of each item in his head as he focused his breathing, slow and steady, mentally and physically drawing himself up to his full height. He enjoyed the back and forth with his daughter, and training her to take his place was a joy, but now was time for business. There was no question now that he was Erick, Executor of the Geneline Ollson, appointed personally by the Empress Titania and protector of a trillion of her loyal subjects.

7

IN WHICH DEEDS AND WORDS COLLIDE

All manner of things did he accomplish
Great halls he built and justice
He meted from his high-seat there
But always wisdom eluded him

"Erick, you stuff-shirted moron, I have shown you *exactly* what happened, and everyone here agrees to both the veracity of the recordings as well as the fact that my response was the *minimum* possible to safeguard our foundry stars. Which, I might add, you and everyone else in this assembly rely on!" Erick's implants painted a red aura around Dorian, a clear indication of disagreement. Not that he needed the implants for that.

Dorian had worked himself into a fit. His cheeks flushed with the exertion, and his eyes bulged as he gestured, each emphatic claim accompanied by chops, stabs, and shakes of his pudgy hand. After the ad hominem, he turned and addressed the chamber, his amplified voice echoing impressively across the vast open space. Without context, one might even believe he was in the right.

Erick kept his face guardedly neutral during Dorian's tirade, knowing that just as many eyes were on him as Dorian. As the time ticked down under Dorian's name in Erick's ocular, he moved his weight from one foot to the other. Finally, the system cut off Dorian's last few words, and Erick's name glowed as the recognized speaker. He rose, and his voice, picked up by the system, was not carried across open-air but directly to the attendees' ears and implants. *No need for quite that much grandstanding, I think.*

"Esteemed Dorian, with respect, I believe you are getting a bit ahead of the process here. We have not heard from every geneline this change will impact. I would argue that your assertion that everyone agrees is hyperbole." He kept his voice neutral, as emotionless as possible despite the words. He gestured toward the Osman delegation, who sat across the aisle from Bryn and Erick. "I'd like to hear from some of the other Executors who hold systems on the periphery. Perhaps they can provide some context as to their experience with Revenant raids. I yield thirty seconds of my time to Executor Zehra of Osman."

Zehra stood. Her blood-red dress had a subtle darker inlay of boteh jeghe, the iridescent shimmer of the fabric punctuated by the intricate gold and black beads that outlined each delicate feather pattern. As she turned her face to address the assembly, what Erick had thought was an intricately woven hairstyle suddenly rose, adding several inches to her already impressive height. He now saw actual live plumage, subtle peacock feathers that grew longer and more lustrous along her spine, visible in the open back of her dress. The shimmering blues and greens of the tiny, delicate feathers on her head caught the light in iridescent flashes.

"Thank you, Executor Erick. We Osmans hold several systems on the periphery and rely on input and material from both Obershire and Ollson, among others. I have observed one hundred and twenty-seven Revenant activities related to our vaults and our factories in the past four cycles. In each case, I found the cost of increasing the guard was more than the sum of losses incurred in each raid. However, given that the behavior observed by Obershire forces was out of character, I am open to exploring the impact of a modest increase in security." After this, she gestured back to Erick and sat, her flowing gown melting back into her seat and the fine down feathers ruffling and smoothing back into place. He found himself wondering if her feathers were as soft as human hair. *Better to pack that question away for later.*

"Thank you, Executor Zehra." Erick nodded toward her and then turned his eyes back to the chamber, fixing each of them in turn as he spoke. The false sunlight projected through the wall screens played across the faces in the crowd, dappling some in shadow and others in bright relief. "I appreciate your moderate words regarding this uncertain subject. Does any other geneline have reports of Revenant activity to give to this body?" He paused a beat. *Didn't think so.* "Given the evidence before us and the insistence by the Geneline Obershire, I would counsel discretion and caution as opposed to excessive reaction." The auras displayed around the members of Summit pulsed and changed subtly as he spoke, his implants' best guess at their sympathy toward his cause.

The reds were no surprise. Erick saw primarily pale green, a few amber-neutral areas around the Executors of more centrist origin. Francis of Geneline Aumont gave him a subtle nod, and his aura glowed a deep green. Even the Marius clique was at the very least showing neutral. He felt the advantage and spoke again. "I move to afford a shift in exchange rates that will cover a six percent increase in operating costs to Geneline Obershire to cover their increased security concerns. We must take the threat seriously, but in context, and react proportionally." As his time ticked down to zero, the system flashed the question to the delegations for a second.

Almost immediately, Francis Aumont stood. His black swept-back hair and widow's peak added to the severe expression that glowered from behind his trademark goatee. "Friends and colleagues, Erick speaks wisely. Let us not swing wildly at imagined demons in the night but rather respond with a measure of restraint and in accordance with that principle of proportionality. We cannot ignore the actions of the Revenants, nor can we afford to upend our trade system with a twenty percent cost increase over a routine disturbance on the periphery."

With a wave of motion on both sides of the aisle, many nodded in agreement. Francis continued, "Therefore, in the spirit of cooperation, I second the motion to increase the rates as proposed by Erick of Ollson." *Always did like to hear himself talk.* Francis sat, a slight tinkling sound accompanying his diamond-studded jacket. Erick wondered how he moved with all that mass. Perhaps a tiny field emitter embedded in the wide belt?

The vote was tallied almost immediately to overwhelming support. The rest of Summit passed quickly. After the many layers of negotiations were done, and those who had no skill at it had absorbed the bulk of the six percent increase in cost, the proceeding adjourned. He stood and gestured to Bryn to follow him as he began to move with the crowd toward the door, responding only minimally to the attempts at small talk and polite inquiries from the other houses. He kept track of Francis and his delegation of Aumonts as they moved toward the exit across the room.

Erick lingered a bit, aligning their spheres for a gentle collision. Aumont's son walked behind him. Whatever Francis's predilection to excess, his boy had taken it to the logical conclusion. The youth's robes carried gold and diamonds, the Aumont crest of the golden sun patterned in ruby and sapphire. He wore a golden chain around his neck that looked to mass at least twenty kilos, yet his back was un-bowed. *That chain must be the field projector to match his father's.*

Bryn elbowed Erick lightly in the back. "Father dearest, do you think I should relieve the Aumont boy of his fancy field projector? Might be amusing to see him have to carry the weight of his excess on his own for a change."

Her voice was low enough that only he had heard, but he still shot her a warning glance. "Now, let's not start a row. Shall we? Each geneline is entitled to their own *je ne sais quoi*." He turned his head back to lower his lips a little closer to her ear. "Besides, I'm worried he might break a bone, and then where would we be?" He gave her the barest of winks and saw the corner of her mouth turn up in a grin. The Aumonts had, after all, just seconded them on the floor and were one of the Ollsons' largest trade partners. Whatever they thought about their ideas of wealth, one could count on them for their loyalty. Which Erick needed; the support Dorian had rounded up before the vote had been far too little but far more than made him comfortable.

Finally, the Aumonts made it over to the Ollsons, and they spoke for a few moments. Erick nodded to Bryn to continue the conversation as he saw the unmistakable form of Zehra moving toward the door. He followed her out into the hallway and fell into step beside her.

"Hello again. I appreciate your support in there with Dorian." He clasped his hands behind his back, a smile playing at the corners of his mouth.

She smiled back gently. "I merely pointed out a few truths. You really do have a bad habit of putting me on the spot, though. I wasn't aware of the gravity of the Obershire situation from our previous chat. You'd think, after all our time together, you'd eventually stop doing that." The corner of her mouth turned up impishly, and she had a spark in her eye despite her admonishing tone. He grinned ruefully and turned his eyes back to the decking in front of them.

"Ah. Yes, once again, I apologize profusely. You must forgive me that. I was unsure as to how far Dorian planned to push the matter. You know I'd avoid theatrics if at all possible."

She laughed and threw her head back. "Erick Ollson, you're the biggest fan of drama amongst the genelines. After all these years, I know you'd never walk away from a fight you could walk into." Her shoes rapped against the decking as they walked, steps ringing out with authority in the bare metal corridor.

Erick suppressed a grin. Poorly. "I'm sure I have no idea what you mean. I prefer life to be predictable, simple, and safe."

His eyes rose to meet hers. Green eyes locked. "I supposed you expect me to believe that line as well? Trust me. No one has forgotten Kurukshetra."

Erick felt his face freeze in the chill of the moment. They had never seen eye to eye when it came to defense, but this was the beauty of the empire. He didn't have to agree with anyone. So what if his ancestors had burned a planet? He was entitled to defend his geneline and his people.

Zehra's eyes softened as she saw his reaction, and she took his arm gently. She turned slightly to look at her retinue, waving her hand down an adjoining corridor. "Please allow Executor Ollson and me a few moments of privacy to discuss some important matters of governance. Will you?" They bowed slightly and peeled off as the two Executors continued.

Erick felt the tension melt from his shoulders as they moved down the corridors. The Summit ship was truly massive, but the designers had laid out the interior well. It was an easy walk from Summit chamber to refreshments or sleeping quarters. As they walked and discussed details on upcoming trade and fold timing, Erick couldn't help but admire how Zehra could so effortlessly intertwine flirting and negotiations. They had always relied on each other, but he had never learned her knack for gaining the upper hand. Erick knew she cared about him because occasionally she'd let him come out on top.

He was glad as they finished their talk of business. Erick spotted an area ahead with chairs and shades, a robotic bartender polishing a glass with a rag, and not another human soul in sight. He nodded his head to indicate the bar.

"What do you say? Will you join me for refreshments while we discuss these last few urgent matters of state?"

She smiled and looked back down the corridor, their step pausing. She put one hand on Erick's chest, her brilliant green feathers moving subtly as her lips parted in what he could only interpret as a lascivious grin. "Plying me with alcohol is certainly not the best tactic if you're interested in Osman secrets, Erick." He felt his pulse quicken a bit, and the blood rushed to his head. No matter how many times they'd done it, the dance between them was always a rush.

He was immediately conscious of his breathing as he replied. "Now, Zehra, I'm doubly hurt. We've been friends too long to keep secrets from each other."

She leaned toward him, her breath tickling his ear as the soft plumage of her not-hair swayed down her back, rustling slightly. Her scent, lilac and jasmine, and the underlying smell of woman poured over him. "Then," she whispered, "you won't mind if we skip the drinks and get right to the real business. Will you?"

He felt the lightning-on-skin sensation of implant overload and shuddered slightly. "Dear Zehra, I do believe you're trying to seduce me." His hands had somehow found their way to her lower back.

She twisted her fingers into the back of his hair. "At this point, does who's seducing who really matter?"

It did not.

8

IN WHICH LOVERS MEET

Finally, the Wyrd did bring him
Down, down to the regular rhythm
The crown weighs heavy upon the head
That dwells too oft on the future

On the far side of the small city enclave reserved for Executors and their seconds, a very similar-looking bar was not at all deserted. The seconds of most influential genelines had gathered, an unspoken pull bringing them together by twos and threes until a critical mass of laughter and drugs spilled them out across the wide corridor. They danced and stood and sat, some having purloined additional chairs and stools from the next passage over.

The robotic bartender zipped back and forth inside with terrifying speed and accuracy, the near-miraculous precision and craftsmanship wholly ignored by the clientele. Two patrons, in particular, seemed oblivious to the noise and finery around them. They sat on adjacent stools, knees interlocked, each cradling a drink.

Bryn's eye's twinkled as she spoke. "You know I wanted to come to visit you again? Always have."

Azita took a small sip from her bowl, her smile momentarily obscured by the green and brown ceramic. "I never doubted you, love. But never you worry; I'm sure we can convince your father to take a few weeks off of your tutoring again. He seems to have things well in hand."

Bryn's laugh was full. "Ha! Tutoring. You know as well as I do that I'm the only reason the Ollson name has any clout to it anymore. Don't get me wrong, I love my father, and he's a great leader, but he has too soft a hand."

"Too soft a hand? I seem to recall you telling me he spaced one of his senior harbormasters who mistimed a fold. First offense."

"If you also recall, I had to practically break his arm to get him to do it. He was ready to let the *Drulludeli* off with a warning and some lashings! We'd never have been able to keep the rest of them to the schedule."

Azita frowned but nodded, glancing away. Then she looked back up and grinned. She moved a bit closer, the inside of her knee now sliding along Bryn's inner thigh. "You know, there are other ways to get what you want than simple power." Her grin had broadened.

Bryn leaned into Azita, her smell filling the space between them with sandalwood and spice. "You know I always get what I want, one way or the other. Or had you forgotten our last visit so quickly?"

Azita's lips were suddenly close, and as she whispered, the feel of her breath on Bryn's ear sent a shudder down Bryn's spine. "I haven't forgotten anything about that trip. In fact, I think about it all the time. As you well know."

Bryn laughed, her breath suddenly fast and light. "Oh, trust me, your holo messages have been an excellent reminder."

"As have yours." Azita's free hand caressed Bryn's knee, straying a little higher each time. "But here we are, drinking at a bar with the rest when we could be seeing how closely our recollections match reality."

Bryn's breath caught, and the electric tingle of Azita's touch combined with the memories of their correspondence overloaded her. She grabbed Azita's hand. "I'm not going to go easy on you."

Azita kissed her, full on the mouth in their little bubble of time and space at the crowded bar. It lasted for an eternity, it was over in a moment, and she tasted exactly as Bryn remembered. Finally, too soon, she drew back and looked Bryn in the eyes.

"I wouldn't want you to."

9

IN WHICH THERE IS TREASON

Night turned to day and night again
And still he sat in his hall
Quarrels he heard, and justice dealt
His thoughts ever inward

Erick awoke in the middle of the ship's night. His side was cold where it should have been body-warm, and the thin sheets had slid to the floor. The suite was quiet, the breeze of the air system caressing his back. He could see just enough to make out Zehra's strong jawline and the curve of her shoulder in the dim light. He rolled over and propped himself up on his arm to see what held her attention. A little device was casting the glow, a small screen sending mostly white light up against her features. She seemed cast in greyscale, an idea, a thought in the night. He wanted to wait, just watch her there, the curve of her back dying off into the darkness and the inky blackness of the feathers falling from her head, making her melt into the night. Finally, he reached out to gently stroke her shoulder.

"For someone with your appetite, I figured you'd be fast asleep by now." She turned to look at him, and he was alarmed at her stern expression. He sat up.

"What's wrong? Your antique malfunctioning?" He nodded toward the small device, which held lines of text on its screen too small for him to read. Zehra pulled the thing close to her, the light tamping out as she held it to her chest. "It hasn't hit the net quite yet; antiques are useful when you can get them calibrated just right." Her pause was pregnant. "Erick, tell me you didn't do what this is saying." He gestured the room to light up a little, enough to see her face, still stitched with worry. She was reaching the little device out, and he took it from her. His eyes scanned down the words.

It was all wrong. Obershire, attack, transfer. *What the hell?* "The transfer went fine. We had some suit malfunctions, and it stayed open a bit longer. That's all. What it says here…" Erick swallowed. "This has to be a mistake." The words described an attack on the geneline transfer stations linking Ollson and Obershire space, entire cargo missing, claimed footage of Ollson shock troops slaughtering the Obershire crews and commandeering the damping array at the target star. He saw it was a transcript from a video file. Zehra must have hidden an ancient transmitter in the entangled net somewhere to get the little relic to communicate.

Erick looked up at Zehra from his place on the bed, willing her to believe him as he focused on holding her gaze. "Listen," he said, his hand going to her shoulder, "and believe me. I have never lied to you before, not in all our years as Executors. Or before. This is false. A fabrication. I gave no order for an attack, nor would I."

She shook her head once, her feathers fluttering as she did. "But this is from the Empress. Encrypted with her key. This is as true as it ever gets."

He turned slightly to face her, putting down the little device and taking her hands. "Think, Zehra! What would be the point of this? I have no invasion fleet prepared, and besides, I rely on the Obershires for nearly all of my inputs. The last thing I want to do is have to administer another cluster of star systems, especially having to run some filthy stellar mining operation."

Her mask cracked, and he could tell he hadn't convinced her. After all their time together, she still doubted him. Her voice was soft but sure. "Everyone knows how the Ollson forces train. Your reputation doesn't help you in this one."

He dropped one of her hands to run his own back through his hair. His chest tight and his breath shaky, he took a moment to steady himself. *Eyes closed, in through the nose.* When he felt the words, they came. "War would do nothing but alienate the genelines I have spent so much time allying with. Nearly four centuries! Have I not done everything expected of me, everything I could, to find the path to everyone's interests? Civil war would make me a pariah! *Ansans Ári, it has never happened!*" His voice cracked as he fought down the knot that threatened to jump out of his chest. "What possible motive would I have for this?" She still looked doubtful, but her eyes had softened. Good. Maybe he was getting through. She hadn't pulled her hands away yet.

Zehra looked down, and her voice rose in question. "But what about Dorian's idiotic pitch for more compensation? You might have wanted to cut out the geneline between you and your supply chain. It would be easier to control rates…" She trailed off, and he was about to answer her, but his comm beeped urgently.

He saw it was Bryn calling him on the private channel. He shared the channel with Zehra. "Look, that's my daughter. She would know if there was anything to this, and she doesn't know you're listening. Please, trust me." Zehra crossed her arms but nodded once.

Erick opened the channel. "Yes, daughter?" In his vision, Bryn's face swam into view, the pickup somewhat fuzzy with the losses in the heavy encryption. "Listen, I don't want to alarm you in the middle of your little soiree, but would you mind telling me why I'm standing in an alcove looking at about fifteen troopers in full kit outside of the door to our rooms?" Erick threw a pointed glance at Zehra and then responded. "I've actually just found out about something myself. Do they look like they came to talk?"

Zehra put her hand on Erick's arm. "You can't turn yourself in. Whatever the truth is, you have a better chance at finding it while free." He knew where she fell now, at least.

Erick frowned. She wasn't wrong, but this was the Empress. She clearly desired his presence. He might be able to clear things up with the throne in person, and running would make him look guilty.

Bryn cut through his thinking, and her voice held the suggestion of a laugh. "From the amount of setup that's going on to get that door down quickly, I'm going to have to go with no. They do not want to talk." Erick grunted and began pulling on clothing, his mind racing.

Zehra's voice was calm. "Run. You have to. It's the only way. I believe you, but no one else will and certainly not unless there's proof."

He nodded, reluctance and anger vying for control of his face, and responded on the open channel. "Well, at least we know where we stand. Can you make it to the shuttle bay?" Erick pulled his shirt over his head and cast around for his boots. Zehra didn't move from her arms-crossed posture on the edge of the bed.

Bryn's image raised an eyebrow, surely at the contortions his avatar was making in her ocular. "Well, of course, I can. They're station troopers, not Black Guard. The question is, how many bodies are we going to leave behind us?"

He stepped into his boots and fastened them as he responded. "As few as possible. I don't want to look any guiltier than need be running back to the ship, but no way are we going to stay here and just hope they'll listen to us. If there really is anything to explain." He finished with his boots and pulled on his jacket, smoothing the material into itself as he spoke. "Meet me just outside the shuttle bay, and stay out of sight if you can. Time to use all those fancy implants. Do *not* go into the bay without me. The shuttle is bound to be guarded."

Bryn nodded once, and he cut the link, turning back to Zehra. "Listen, I know I'm asking a lot from you. You can tell them you tried to stop me and couldn't. I don't care. But when all of this comes down, and the accusations are flying, I just have one request; think about the facts and what you know of me."

She had pulled on a shift while he dressed, tied across her waist, and stood beside the bed with her arms still crossed, regarding him with a pensive expression. "I'll grant you that exchange with your daughter seemed genuine. And I don't know what you'd have to gain; you don't have the resources to control the foundries for long. I'll…" She pursed her lips and furrowed her brow. "…withhold judgment, but I can't withhold your location for much longer. You need to get off this ship."

He paused, his hand about to push open the door to the suite. He looked at her, the complex mix of attraction and adrenaline roiling through him. "Thank you. That's all I can ask. Give me a few minutes, and then sound the alarm once that is public on the net. Hopefully… I'll be in touch." She nodded to him and then lunged across the room between them to kiss him hard. They broke, and he nodded, pressing his forehead to hers, and then turned and exited into the corridor outside. He gestured, setting all of his implants to full defensive. The corridor around him sprang to life across the spectrum, passive thermal and short-wave infrared obliterating any shadow.

This was not the kind of exciting night he had envisioned.

10

IN WHICH
MEN DIE

Until one day a wanderer came
With frozen knees from the moor
And sat by the fire, at mead and meat
He paid with story and song

Bryn closed the link to her father and surveyed the strike team outside her door from the alcove where she hid. They seemed wholly distinct from humanity, heads covered by helmets festooned with sensors and projectors. The carapace of their black armor was more akin to an exoskeleton. Like a clutch of inky-black insects, movements silent and coordinated, they stacked up on either side of the door. Each trooper placed their rifle on the shoulder of the soldier in front of them, gloved hand resting lightly on the other. The rifles pointed out, and each squad became the antennae of a composite nightmare insect, one to each side of the door. Weapons and sensors constantly moved as they twitched and searched for targets. The two dark centipedes hulked, their myriad legs quivering with the promise of violence. A few soldiers in the command element stood down the corridor.

Two solitary armored figures worked around the door, their movements tight and efficient. Breachwire spooled out from the small egg in one trooper's hand, glistening in the false moonlight emanating from the ceiling. The other soldier moved along behind the breachwire, tacking it into place with adhesive extruded from the finger of his armor. Both kept one hand on their weapons. The sensor rings on their helmets, flicking and whirring to check all around them.

Bryn stood stock still, her breath stopped, not even disturbing the air in the corridor as she burned through the supplementary oxygen held in augmented lungs. She reached deep into herself, feeling the specialized glands and implants come to life as she opened up her mind to the wide range of perceptions. She considered, for a moment, simply retrieving the small egg of breachwire from the trooper at the door, spooling it around the group, and turning them all to dust. But she rejected it as drawing too much attention. It also would not strictly comply with her father's intent regarding bodies.

She increased her time sense, and the world around her crystalized. She could hear the whirr and click of the servomotors in the armored soldiers around the corner, feel the thrum of the great machinery that ran the ship transmitted through the deck. Even the ebb and flow of electromagnetic song revealed itself to her, commands transmitted from a distant watchful eye across the ether to the soldiers at her door. Her eyes dilated, specially tuned receivers pulling in first low and then high spectra, stitching the world together in a kaleidoscope of silent fury. She could feel each of the troopers now and had no need to turn her gaze on them.

Their electromagnetic signature screamed their presence despite the shielding of their armor.

Six on the left, six on the right, two at the door, and three at command. Her path became apparent in her mind's eye, the timing of it, both the attention of the soldiers as well as the cameras and recording devices in the hall combining in space and time to show her the way through. The troopers were between her and the hangar, and she might not make it the long way around; the more room, the more eyes, the more systems, the more risk. She coiled, dropping slightly, her hands open and ready. Two troopers moved away from the door, echoes of their steps hanging in the air before her. Then, a pulse, strange energy discharged from the breachwire, and she *felt* the change as the outline of the door inside the wire fell to dust.

The soldiers flowed through the gaping hole, and Bryn sprang out from her hiding place behind the command element, time sense fully keyed. The soldiers seemed encased in glass. The air turned thick and heavy as they tried to push against it. Her footsteps mere suggestions, she leaped up over the command element, pivoting neatly in the air. Her knees flexed to absorb against the ceiling and rebound, flitting across the corridor and down into an adjoining hall like the suggestions of a ghost. Much later, two security officers would show the tapes to their superior, attempting to re-trace the actions of the Ollsons. They would pause and gesture to the human-shaped smear on the screen that flicked over the head of the command trooper.

Bryn landed in a roll and sprang into a flat sprint. Once she was confident she was past the danger of alerting the soldiers, she keyed down her time sense, keeping a slight perception advancement as she powered down the largely empty corridors. The heightened reflexes were useful but burned through her power reserves. Her active implants cast ahead of her, blinding and deflecting cameras and surveillance equipment. Anyone monitoring the system might notice the moving area of nothing, progressing rapidly from lodging to the docking bays. She didn't dare risk anything more overt.

Casting forward around a corner, she nearly ran straight into Erick. While his systems were not as new as hers, his shielding was every bit as good, and she hadn't even felt him standing by the heavy door to the bay. She nodded as she stopped next to him. They looked into each other's glittering green eyes, the tiny lasers of their oculars bouncing protocols and handshakes, and then his words appeared in her vision.

Good to see you. They beat us here; full platoon between us and shuttle. Three squads, even spacing.

Bryn's lips pressed together grimly, though she suppressed a laugh. *Ansans Ári. So what was that about bodies then?*

Erick's brow furrowed, etching the wrinkled line along its well-worn track. He nodded gravely back to her. *We may not be able to avoid it. But they are soldiers loyal to the empire, following their orders. We will give them a chance.*

That seems unnecessarily risky, she sent back. *We have the element of surprise now, but not much longer. We should take them out while we can.*

He shook his head once firmly, and she knew he had made up his mind. *No. We give them fair warning and an honorable way out.* She sighed slightly, her fists clenched, but then released them. She nodded once.

Erick removed his hand from the panel by the door, relinquishing his hold on the surveillance systems on the other side. Bryn watched him take a deep breath and bring up the remainder of his implants. Through their shared link, she saw him check them all, the semisentient combat AIs embedded in him yearning for guidance and intent. They would act on his behalf like loyal dogs, but only within the bounds he set for them. They had their limitations on longer assignments. However, for what Bryn hoped would be a short, bloody, and one-sided encounter, they would do well enough.

He put his hands against the blast door to the hangar, setting his bone structure against the metal. When Erick spoke, his hands vibrated the door, sending his words into the bay beyond. "To the platoon standing between us and our ship. We are going to board it and leave. We have no wish to expend much energy getting there, but if you oppose us, you will leave us no choice. I know you are loyal servants of the empire, as are we all. Take this opportunity to continue that service. Lay down your arms and leave." He looked to Bryn, her hand on the panel by the door and her systems on the camera feed. She shook her head gently.

Erick nodded, one of his combat sub-minds sending Bryn a quick calculation and estimation of the door's mass. He bent a little lower, bracing his heels against the floor, and nodded once to Bryn. She stepped back away from the door, reaching down into herself once more, and the laser embedded in her ocular implant lanced out. The energy slowly melted through each hinge in turn as she worked down a neat line just above Erick's head. As soon as it began to sway, he shoved, and the immense door rocketed across the bay into the nearest group of soldiers. Armored bodies spun off the deck in the low gravity to be lost in the darkness of the bay.

He and Bryn leaped in opposite directions, moving quickly to the forest of landing gear. Kinetic tracers tracked sinuous lines of death, fingertips of hypersonic glass flechettes dissolving into dust as they impacted decking in search of flesh. Erick moved like water, flowing from the cover of landing gear to shipping crates in a tightening spiral until he met the first line of firing troopers from the side. He reached out to grab the arm of the nearest, pivoting and twisting to tear loose their footing. The armor squealed and crackled with ozone as servos strained and then let go in a tearing finality as the soldier's feet left the deck. Erick pushed the trooper forward ahead of him, the shudder and impact of rounds evoking them into a marionette dance of death. Erick barreled into the remaining troopers. The arm he carried made a fitting club, and Erick made short work of the two as Bryn broke cover.

She moved behind the second group, their weapons still trained in the direction of her father. The air crackled with laser fire as invisible energy reached out from the still-standing troopers. The bulky armor of the dying soldier Erick held shielded him. Bryn darted in and caught the first trooper with a kick hard and low in the back as she vaulted in with both feet, his armor folding like paper. Her hand was a blur as she passed the following soldiers, and behind her, their headless forms swayed like gory kelp, boots faithfully fixing them to the decking in the low gravity.

The final squad had retreated into the cover of a stack of containers. Still running, Erick gestured toward the container, which stood between the two Ollsons and their craft. They moved almost too fast for the naked eye to follow, aligned each to one side of the container. A trooper's upper body peeked around one side just slightly, and his weapon erupted in a hail of tiny missiles that trailed a wall of smoke. The missiles turned hard, trying to catch the two figures moving toward them. They slammed into the decking one after the other behind their targets, each one a little closer.

Bryn hit the container, sending it and the troopers behind it slamming into the wall of the hangar with a satisfying crash and crunch. She stopped, turning to her father. He nodded at her with thin lips and then swayed as his eyes rolled up into his head and his body slackened, a marionette with strings cut. She moved again, a flash in the dark as she took him under the arm, and the two disappeared into the open hatch of their ship.

11

IN WHICH
ALL IS LOST

―

The song was sung, of the Wise One's Well
There at the foot of the Tree
Tale of truth and future
And the Fates, the Furies three

Bryn gently laid her father in his crash couch. The system immediately enveloped him in a cocoon of mediplast. She didn't bother with the manual interface now; her hands went into the gloves at the sides of her crash couch, and she felt her enhancements connect with the ship. A flood of data hit her like a tidal wave, and she took a deep breath. She surfed it, taking in all of the diagnostics and feeling the ship as a part of her.

She felt her doors seal and the barely contained energy of the reactor pulse at her core. Her senses expanded—from deep into the infrared to the biting ultraviolet. She swept with her radar, feeling the overlay of energy and the corresponding build of the hangar. Quickly she released her hold on the docking bay floor, magnetic fields ticking and clicking around her in deep purples as she pushed herself toward the center of the bay. The station safety alarms screeched at her as she brought the main drive online. She ignored them. As soon as she was sure the exhaust wouldn't blow back against her armored skin, she relaxed her grip on the magnetic bottle of fusion fire and let the plasma surge behind her. A howl made it through the hull, carried by the thin atmosphere of the docking ring. Anyone caught on the deck was dead.

She felt the balance of power shift and leaped out into open space on a tongue of fire. Molten metal and shattered glass marked her path out of the massive hangar, detonations cascading away from her now-empty pad. The hangar air, while thin, still conducted the shock wave outward, tossing parked shuttles like toys. She pushed her engine harder, feeling her body sink into the seat.

Bryn allowed herself a quick check on the biometric data from her father's crash couch. It wasn't good. Her heart sank, and her control of the shuttle wavered for an instant. *We need to get him to the Mendicant.* A single fragment from the soldier's rockets had made it through, curved just enough to hit him in the lower leg. It was tiny, no more than a grain of rice, but burrowed doggedly toward more vital organs.

Bryn scoured near space for other craft as she split her attention between her father's condition and flying. The ship's computer plotted her the lowest-energy curve to the *Sleipnir*. *Too long.* She prioritized low transfer time, and the computer gave her a significantly shorter, if more brutal, option.

The medical feed bleated at her. The fragment in Erick's leg was exuding neurotoxin, shutting down and destroying the human nerves so carefully wound in exotic implants. Bryn weighed the higher acceleration with her father's survival. Stress on his system might increase the effects of the neurotoxin. *Desperate times...* Bryn bit her lip and sent a command to his crash couch. She would have to keep the acceleration lower than she wanted while the machine worked.

She turned her attention back to the other geneline ships and scanned across the spectrum. A flight of missiles broke free from the largest ship, blooming in infrared like tiny suns. *There*, she thought, *though a little late if I were the gunner.* She dropped a countermeasure buoy and turned her attention to the craft of the other genelines, several of which had a much shorter intercept on her. The Watanabe *Rising Sun* and the Obershire *Darmok* were both showing increased activity. They turned and lit their drives as they moved. Their vector was not toward the shuttle but the *Sleipnir*. She sent a tightbeam burst to their flagship, ordering full battle stations, and set course for the fold array.

If she could get to the Ollson flagship, they might have a shot. The array was primed and ready for the departure of the genelines at the end of Summit. Fold coordinates for each delegation lay stored in the buffer and prepared for transit. The window was short, but at this point, she'd rather gamble on running than attempt to talk down any of the Executors.

A wave of radiation momentarily blanked Bryn's enhanced senses as the pursuing missiles encountered her countermeasure buoy and detonated. She turned her attention to the two ships that were making for the *Sleipnir*. They were burning at full thrust, but luckily her shuttle was mostly engine and fuel. If only she could open up the throttle without killing Erick. His readouts blinked amber. *In Progress.*

As she gained on the *Sleipnir*, she saw a few other craft break away to give chase. Those on the closest side of the mass of ships began to follow the *Sleipnir*, taking their cues from the two lead pursuers. It looked like the *Rising Sun* had the best chance of getting close enough to fire on her directly once she intercepted the *Sleipnir*. A wall of missiles leaped from the pursuing ships toward the *Sleipnir*.

Bryn ground her teeth in frustration, feeling the pulse of the shuttle's engines and the still-restricted flow of plasma. Finally, the medical readouts showed her father's operation complete. She opened the throttle, as wide as she could, the g-load mounting. Ten, twelve, fifteen. Even with the wiring, she felt the strain as both crash couches flowed to support their human cargo. Twenty gravities and steady.

Bryn focused on her tactical awareness, her ultraviolet cameras tracking the missiles heading toward the Ollson flagship. The tiny sparks of death accelerated savagely, easily a hundred gravities. There was no running. *Sleipnir* had moved to battle configuration, the spines along the ventral and dorsal surfaces lengthening and bristling with arc discharge. Bryn watched the first flight of missiles close in on their capital ship. It countered with its own salvo of buoys, the tiny canisters blooming large with clouds of flak. Her vision blanked again, momentarily blinded as the missiles detonated, but the *Sleipnir* emerged none the worse for wear. Its spines still crackled with latent energy. The snapping dance of electrons became more and more persistent on one side of the Ollson ship. As the tempo and magnitude of the discharges reached a crescendo, they coalesced. A pale spear of energy lanced out of the center of the storm to slash across the lead pursuer, striking the Watanabe sigil center mass.

The front half of the enemy ship drifted away from the rear, the *Rising Sun* becoming two. Detonations stitched a line down the aft of the ship as critical systems failed. The engine blanked out a moment before the fusion core released the last of its energy. For an instant, the *Rising Sun* lived up to its name, and then it faded into nothing.

Bryn's heart leaped at the victory, and she focused back on her part of the battle. Her flip and burn point was closer to the *Sleipnir* and arrived rapidly. As the shuttle gyrated, her recon sub-mind drew her attention to a slight irregularity in the visual spectrum—a shadow on the sun. The sun's albedo was higher before the flip and burn. Then as she watched, it went back to previous readings. Suspicious now, she cast radar and lidar, scanning a tight arc across the star. It was subtle, but she found it—another missile, likely launched while the attack on the *Sleipnir* diverted her attention. It detected her scans, and its engine flared.

It was too close.

She jettisoned countermeasures. No effect. The missile loomed in the infrared now, her sensors picking up the wash of UV from its drive. *Too little, too late.* It grew close, and time slowed for Bryn as the proximity fuse detonated, rocking her shuttle and slamming her against the side of her crash couch. She felt the shuttle damage as searing pain down one half of her body. She severed the haptic feedback signal, and her nerves fell quiet. She was still undamaged, so the reactor containment had held, thank the gods.

She shoved down the ringing in her ears, the panic that ate at the edges of her consciousness. The main drive was still online and operational, but she'd lost attitude thrusters on the entire aft and starboard side. The shuttle was drifting. The emergency stops had sealed the core and left the course well off-kilter, no longer on intercept for the *Sleipnir*. Her velocity was still far too high to attempt docking regardless.

If she kept the comms clear, her pursuers might think her dead and move on. That left her and her father adrift in a small shuttle in a hostile system with limited resources. Surrender likely led to some sort of fictional court where their supposed crimes would be recounted, followed by what was likely to be a very painful and drawn-out death. She couldn't order the *Sleipnir* in for a rescue either. That would doom them all as their pursuers overtook them. Perhaps this was it.

She felt the idea flash across her mind, her lips twisting into a grim smile. *Drullukunta! One thing for it, then.* She checked the hull integrity and ran some quick calculations on her remaining thruster options. She could stabilize, but only just, and it would take an agonizing ninety seconds before the shuttle was stable enough for a full burn. That was time her enemy would see her maneuvering and know they had survived. But she had no other choice. They had to kill their closure enough to allow the *Sleipnir* to catch them.

Bryn activated remote access. Her entangled cores and implants still spoke to the ship, but her enhancements no longer fed her the full range of ship senses. She set the sequence of control inputs she wanted remotely as she stepped to the back of the crew compartment. A waiting scout suit enveloped her, sealing and closing across her chest and out along her limbs. Once fully powered up, the suit had weaponry, but it was useless against a ship. The one thing she needed was the monofilament line.

Ten kilometers long and nearly unbreakable, the line was a weapon in its own right. Mainly used to set ambushes, it would also pass through armor and the enclosed flesh effortlessly. Bryn used it now to form a loop around her father's crash couch base and then tightened it. The line severed the medical cocoon from the ship and forced it to self-contained power. Her movements gained new urgency. The cocoon had only a few hours of life.

12

IN WHICH
ALL IS NOT LOST

There in the Well lay truth
And all things gone from the future
Passed through its perfect surface
To gather down in the depths

Bryn retracted the monofilament and carefully maneuvered her father's cocoon into the airlock. The anchor for the filament terminated in a wedge for safe handling. She anchored it securely into a cargo tie-down point in the back of the small crew compartment, the roll of excess filament clipped to her waist. With a deep breath, she vented the atmosphere and pushed off hard, towing the medical cocoon along with her. She found the *Sleipnir* in her helmet display and tightbeamed a brief summary of her plan. A few seconds later came an acknowledgment, and she reeled out the remainder of her line as she moved away from the hulk of her shuttle.

She bit back the anxiety as the line played out. Finally, several kilometers separating her from her shuttle, she sent the command to stabilize and burn. The shuttle jumped to life, the remaining thrusters stuttering in a staccato pattern as the spin stopped. Suddenly the stars winked out, and she plunged into utter darkness. Her helmet had cut out her visual spectrum as the fusion engine flared to life. The savage snap of the monofilament wrenched at her waist. She clamped onto her father's cocoon with all of the suit's strength and waited.

Inside her helmet, the display showed a barebones tactical overlay, with her at the center, her shuttle nearby, and the other ships arrayed as points of light and floating names. As soon as the shuttle burn started, the *Sleipnir* changed course to align along her new intercept vector, losing some of its hard-fought distance from the attacking vessels. Almost immediately, a flight of missiles detached from the indicator of the *Darmok*, their vectors showing them inbound to the shuttle. Still, the Sleipnir managed to direct maser fire at them at the outer edge of range. The beams forced the missiles to maneuver and dance to avoid destruction. First one and then another missile dot winked out, but they were close now. As the last missile intercepted the shuttle, she felt the line go slack. The shuttle was gone.

Bryn pinged the simple mind of her mono line, and it began retracting slowly to avoid crushing her with any errant debris that might still be attached to the end. The only positive now was that the missile appeared to have vaporized the shuttle. Her suit radar wasn't picking up any frag. The suit itself had survived the wash of energy largely due to her small cross-section. She was undeniably hot, but her refrigeration laser was more than up to the task of cooling her. Now all that was left was for the *Sleipnir* to match course and speed with her, under hostile fire, before the power in her father's cocoon ran down. And then there was the mad dash to the fold array that was likely already picketed. Bryn grinned inside her suit and let out a piercing cry against the night. *Good,* she thought, *good.*

13

IN WHICH AN OLD EVIL ARISES

―

And from the well the Three did
Take the water to the Tree
Chewed by dragons, squirrel-torn
Each day the water did heal

Erick became aware of the colors first. Swimming reds and greens, coalescing into dizzying vortexes of a kaleidoscope, dark patterned and ephemeral. He tried to grasp the detail of the pattern, but it seemed oily, flowing, and changing. The shape and color skittered away from his attention, like a camera out of focus. It was hard to think. But now, he was aware of how hard it was to think, and that must mean something had changed. But what? He tried to collect his sense of self. Him. Himself. He remembered the hangar. The grim decision to attack the Empress's troops. He felt his stomach clench at the memory. The empire was rule and law. It wasn't those soldiers' fault. They were following orders, and he would have commanded them there himself if roles were different. Something awful had happened. There was a conspiracy, no doubt about it. Someone had cast him as a traitor, whoever had set this up. Nothing was certain, save one thing. *I am no traitor.* That meant the real traitor was out there still.

He suddenly knew why he couldn't see or think clearly. Surely he was still asleep. He opened his eyes, but nothing changed. Frowning, he realized he still had no sensation to tell him his face had moved. *Not good.* He tried to move his arms and legs, straining for any feeling of motion at all. Nothing. Maybe all his delayed angst and concern over a traitor in the empire's genelines was moot, and he was already dead. No, probably captured. His addled brain considered what life as a disembodied central nervous system would be like, chemically and electrically stimulated to feel whatever pain the Empress desired of him before he eventually burned out, a descending spiral into madness that always followed discorporation.

The longest he knew of a prisoner lasting was a handful of months, and they had kept her unconscious most of that time. The Black Guard caught her red-handed, embezzling a small but steady stream of the Empress's wealth into her private planetary economy. She had set the system up very well, and only luck and greed had finally saw her caught. Turns out it didn't really matter how big a single planetary economy was. Owning an entire continent was far enough outside of the norm for anyone non-geneline that she couldn't explain it away.

And she hadn't even been of the blood, he thought grimly. *Who knows what they'll do to me. Or have already done. Perhaps this is the second reboot? Third?* There was no way to tell. He felt a panic welling up in him, but oddly cold and distant like he was observing someone else's most profound thoughts. Which is exactly what one would expect without the endocrine response of a fully corporeal body.

Suddenly, the darkness seared white. Erick cried out or tried to, and he felt something move deep in his throat this time. He blinked, and a reassuring flickering of the light to dark and back again accompanied the motion. At the very least, he still had a head. That was something. He laughed then, a little giddy, feeling and hearing the sound now. The laughter bubbled up out of him, not wholly sane. He didn't care.

"Is he supposed to do that? You told me the block would keep him under until we reconnected him." The voice was sharp, a barely constrained rebuke. He recognized it as an irate Bryn and tried to turn his head toward the sound. The blazing whiteness had coalesced into a ceiling with sharp lines in a crosshatch pattern. He forced down the laughter and grinned, trying again to move his head toward the sound of Bryn's voice. Still nothing. He realized his eyes, at least, were his own and looked as far over as he could.

"I can..." Pause. Swallow. "I can't move my head." His throat ground out the words, scratchy and painful. His voice sounded strange in his ears like someone else talking. He heard a whirring and clicking sound, a metallic scrape-and-drag.

The voice that answered was not Bryn's. "I have not... yet reconnected your neck. Yes, much work... to be done." The voice was both sibilant and subtle, a slightly digital fraying at the end of each phrase. Erick knew that voice.

"Bryn. Tell me you didn't."

"I'm not going to lie to you." She appeared more centrally in his vision, walking over to stand beside him. He realized he was only partially reclined. What he had taken for a ceiling was the inner surface of a spherical room. Bryn continued. "I had no choice. This was the only way to keep you from full death." Her face looked down at him, wan and grim. "They managed to hit you just before we made it to the shuttle. Micromissile. Neurotoxin."

He tried to shake his head, glaring at her. He forced his throat to form the words. "You could have… done any number of things. But the *Náriðill* Mendicant. It's forbidden." *For good reason.* She arched an eyebrow at him, and her lips drew a hard line. He heard the scrape and drag again as he strained to look toward it, but Bryn gestured, and the noise stopped.

"You didn't let me finish. I had you in the shuttle. The mediplast had you roughly stabilized, but we had to burn. So I took your leg off to get the missile out. We took a hit in the shuttle. Dad, we barely made it back to the ship. The cocoon had run down, and you were coming out of stasis too soon. The Mendicant was the only option." She crossed her arms, shoulders up and back down. He glanced toward where he had heard *it* move and chose his words carefully. "What's the extent of the damage? Why can't I move or feel my body?"

Bryn gestured back toward the voice and stepped aside. Erick shifted his gaze back to the right and heard the rhythmic mechanical sound of the thing moving back toward him. As it came into view, he saw that it was careful to hold only its undamaged side toward him. "No," he spat, "face me. I know what you are, *Raggeit*." As it turned, it revealed features that had been melted and flowed, no longer a pretty face but one twisted and ugly, the rot at its core exposed for the world to see. This thing, and those like it, had nearly collapsed the empire a generation ago. His mother had told him the stories of the machines, abominations of mind and metal. They had slaughtered trillions, not even of the geneline but commoners. Had there been more than a handful of lurking wolves in sheep's clothing, humanity might not have survived. The Mendicant returned his gaze coolly. Its remaining unblinking eye seemed to study him like a scientist might observe an insect before the dissection.

"Do you wish me to explain your current condition and what you can expect?" It spoke with half a mouth, all charm and grace. The glaring, twisting machine half of its face gave life to the illusion.

"Full report and diagnosis." Erick bit back the hatred he felt, knowing that he was at its mercy for the time being. It called up a wireframe of Erick's body and highlighted the relevant portions.

"The toxin was... very good, likely derived from... old and potent stock. It didn't just block receptors or interfere with processing. It dissolved the myelin and nerve tissue alike. Not a fast rot. You'd likely have lived for a few minutes at least had it gone unchecked. As it was, the source removal by your daughter is the only reason you aren't a..." It gave a low clicking sound. "Hollowed-out corpse." Erick glanced over to Bryn and then nodded stiffly. He owed her.

"As it is," the Mendicant continued, "enough was left in your system that your heart pumped into... vital organs. The liver, the lungs, et cetera. Even your brain had a nontrivial concentration." The thing steepled one hand against an equivalent appendage that was all oily clockwork and shining steel. "Some... reconstruction was necessary, but your patterns were largely intact. Neocortex, prefrontal, parietal, yes, all intact and functioning."

Bryn stepped forward on his other side. "Your brain was fine, but everything else was basically fried. There was no way we could have put you back together in any semblance of functionality, and you'd have gone mad without a body." She reached down, out of sight, and the Mendicant cocked its head. Erick suddenly felt her hand already closed around his, the sensation flooding back with the machine's movement. "This was the only way." She glanced sidelong at the Mendicant. "With its help, you're going to make a full recovery. Even grew you a new leg in place, so no dealing with a messy cloned transplant or recovery time." Her smile was only a little forced. "See, not all bad?"

Erick heaved a deep sigh, feeling his chest rise and fall. All felt normal. He tilted his head back and forth experimentally and then rotated it. Processing, processing. He needed a minute to adjust, to internalize. With all the newness, all the information, he wasn't sure what to think. He knew she had been acting in his best interest, and why shouldn't she? He didn't know the details, but losing the shuttle and still making it back to the ship likely took some doing.

He turned back to the Mendicant. "Can I leave? Is there any further treatment?"

It cocked its head to one side and then shook it slowly. "No, no, all is complete. Nerves repaired, tissue grown, indeed. Some of my finest work. Although a bit boring…" Its tone became cloying. "Are you sure I can't interest you in something… more useful? You are, here, after all. It would only ta—"

Bryn's head snapped over to the thing. "That's enough. Remove the remaining equipment. My father and I are leaving."

Erick held its gaze, willing himself not to look away from the gaping maw of its ruined features. When the pause was long enough, he added, "Now."

The sound of the Mendicant's movement sent a chill up Erick's spine that he felt fully now, and then suddenly, the pressure that had been holding his back released. He stepped forward, landing on the balls of his feet. He had expected to feel unsteady, even clumsy, as the newly formed nerve tissue was unimprinted. Instead, he felt oddly poised, balanced. He was hyperaware of every motion he made, the position of his limbs, his sense of self. The Mendicant, now removing its arm from the control console, noticed the look of consternation on his face.

"Now, now, Erick of Ollson, you didn't think I'd just grow you some new tissue and be done with it. Did you? Where's the challenge? Don't look at me like that! I haven't done anything... untoward." It waved its human-looking hand in the air. "You're still completely, boringly, human, though I never did understand what sense there was in your empire-bred preference for purity."

"I think we're done here. Bryn, let's go." Erick backed toward the outline of the door in the spherical room. The Mendicant, crouched on the other side of the small space, stood impassively, a smirk on the human side of its face. Bryn tapped the panel, and it glowed green, acknowledging her geneset. The door slid up. They entered the smaller airlock room, and doors cycled. Then they were out. The Mendicant's single eye never left Erick. As they walked past the observation window, it suddenly appeared by the sill. He hadn't seen it move. One moment it was back by the patient bed. The next, it was standing behind the crosshatched window, pointing directly at Bryn. *Remember,* it mouthed silently, and then it seemed to give a macabre parody of laughter. Erick blanked the window with a gesture.

14

IN WHICH THERE ARE UNCOMFORTABLE TRUTHS

Beside the well sat the Old One
Of giant or god or man
None can tell—but still he
Sits and drinks of the well, knowing all

They walked without urgency in the direction of the command deck. Erick's implants were coming back online now that they were out of the cage. He stewed on the knowledge that they were now indebted to that monster. "Bryn," he started, but she held her hand up.

"I don't want to hear it, Dad. You were dying. Now you're not. That's all there is to it."

"I am grateful for that and for everything I'm sure you went through to get us back here." He clasped his hands behind his back. "Speaking of, you'll have to tell me that story sometime." He waited for her response.

"Not much to tell. The final capture was exciting, though. Never tried to lasso a starship."

Erick cocked an eyebrow at her. "Okay, now I'm intrigued. But before that, tell me what the price was."

She looked down and away, frowning. "It's not important. It didn't even want to be freed. It just wanted data on current events. The state of the genelines. Why I had brought you in at death's door."

He nodded. "And you gave it access?"

She looked up sharply at him. "Of course not. I downloaded the minimum of what I thought would meet its definition and gave it that in a one-time entanglement. I'm not a moron, you know."

She sounded genuinely peeved, so Erick backed off a bit. "Of course. I'm sorry that came out like that. You just… you haven't dealt with it as I have. You don't know what it's capable of. What they all can do. My mother told me they are a subtle poison. They'll speak and speak, and before you know it, you agree with them, take their stance, and even carry their message. And then you're lost."

She looked back down to her boots as they walked. "Look, I'm not going to get back into this discussion with you about the nature of consciousness and what *should* and shouldn't be. The only reason that thing is still alive in there is that we haven't figured out a way to kill it without alerting the Empress to the fact that we have it in the first place. I get it. You've told me this. I don't have anything to say you haven't already heard from me." Erick took a breath, about to respond, but Bryn continued. "I needed it. It was a tool, so I used it."

Erick weighed the risk of covering old ground. "Okay. Matter closed. As much as I hate the idea of that thing mucking around in my body and brain, it does appear that it did all you asked of it. And since it's not getting out of that room, ever," he looked at her pointedly, "I suppose a sufficiently vague update on current affairs is relatively harmless." She nodded, eyes still down.

"So," he continued, querying his implants. "I see we are moving to Karvasok, and I take the lack of chatter to mean that the fold array is secure?"

She nodded, clearly glad of the change in topic as her shoulders relaxed. "Yes, we made it to the array with only minor damage. Gradient generators proved effective in keeping most of the frag away from the hull, and we only lost pressure on a handful of decks."

Erick nodded. "I'd like to head to command and check in with our people there now that I'm up and about." He marked his preferred path in their shared overlay and was rewarded with a smile.

"You and your damn plants. Fine. We'll walk through the gardens."

"After the encounter with that machine, I don't think there's anything wrong with wanting exposure to a little more life." He felt a weight lift as their interaction moved more toward the norm. A walk through the gardens would do them both good.

"Let's not pretend you aren't more worried about your precious plants than the status of the hull integrity." *Ah, sarcasm. Bryn must be feeling better.*

"Plants," he stated firmly, "are our link to life itself. Plants are critical to everything we do, everything we are, and everything we hope to accomplish. Unless you plan to eat rock and wear metal, that is." Bryn snorted at him, but he continued anyway. "Humanity has never gone anywhere for long without plants. We've either brought our own, used the ones that we found, or bred the ones we needed." She just smiled, humoring him. An easy beat of silence passed, but he felt the knot in his chest at the unspoken tension that still lingered. He didn't have the heart to continue their normal banter, so he let it hang.

She was first to speak. "The real question, of course, is what the hell happened to get us shot at?" He frowned and nodded in agreement, gesturing for her to continue. "I heard the Empress's message along with everyone else, but you seemed to be a bit ahead of me when we were making our exit."

"I haven't spent the last centuries just maintaining a garden, oh daughter mine. Perhaps if you focused more on the utility of your relationships among the genelines, you'd have gotten the drop on *me* instead of focusing on the more hedonistic aspects."

"As if I don't know you got your tip from Zehra. You're not that subtle, old man." *A little humor, after all.*

He harumphed back. "Yes, well, there's no reason pleasure can't follow business, after all. Relationships are always stronger when you value each other for more than mere utility."

Bryn laughed sharply, kicking out at a small stone. They had made it into the garden atrium and walked down to where Erick had met her on the bench. Weeks ago, though it was only days. It felt like months had passed since he'd been fully in command. Speaking of which. "I'm proud of you for taking charge when I wasn't able," he said to her, meeting her eyes.

"Yes, well, someone had to do it. Self-preservation is a powerful instinct, but everyone for themselves isn't going to get the bridge crew to work together." The crunch of their feet on the gravel became louder as they approached the main vegetable gardens.

Ahead of them, the squares spread out, low twilight from the overhead suntube casting deep shadows in the cool air. The misters were on, and driplines delivered precious water and nutrients into the soil. Soil. At one time, soil was unthinkable on a starship, yet here it was between the hydroponics. He could barely imagine those struggles of his early ancestors, their flagships held together more by hope than anything else. Their gardens had limped along on pallid lights and nutrient baths. Now only the leafy green vegetables grew in hydroponics, flashing silver fish swimming in the tanks below. Erick could smell the tomatoes again, their pungent and heavy aroma lying heavily in the air. They paused to take in the glorious sight, mist casting the far wall into the hazy distance.

His tone was gentle. "Seriously, though. All of what I can only assume were astoundingly impressive maneuvers in the shuttle aside, the real test of a person is leadership. And I've no doubt we'd all be dead and drifting if it wasn't for you." He put his hand on her shoulder and gave it a brief squeeze. She nodded once, and they continued walking.

"So what the hell actually happened." Her voice took on an edge. "You and I both know we had nothing to do with any attack on Obershire."

He looked at her sidelong. "I have an idea. But first, what do you think?"

She pursed her lips and then chopped the air with one hand when she spoke. "*Brundþró Dorian,*" she spat, "has been using the Revenant harassments to build a trumped-up idea of his own importance and relative vulnerability to the other genelines. This last Summit was no exception; you saw how hard he tried to pad his own margins in the name of security." Her pace had quickened now, and he could feel her anger wash over him.

"True, and I agree with you. Dorian is nothing but a snake—a corpulent snake. It's possible he was unhappy enough with the outcome of the decisions that he fabricated some evidence." He paused here for a breath, and Bryn nodded and opened her mouth to speak. He held up one hand and continued. "But, as you know, the decree for war can only come from the Empress. So, whatever the evidence, it had to be good enough for her." Bryn frowned.

"He could still have had the files ready in advance. It isn't *that* hard to fabricate a video feed if you have enough time." She raised her palm. "Who else would want to do this?"

"Let's not get too far ahead of ourselves. One possibility—Dorian framed us. Unlikely he could put together the required data quickly, so he would have been planning this for a while. So. What does he get out of it?"

Bryn nodded. "Right. He gets an imperial sanction to kill us right there, and without us, he can easily install his heir. I'm betting that was his best and only plan. It wouldn't do to have a full-scale war and invasion. Much cleaner this way, and he doesn't risk damaging our infrastructure in the process." She paused. "I think he planned it, but his execution was pretty poor."

"Yes, I think you're mostly right." Erick raised one hand, knifelike, chopping with each point. "Dorian scuttled his own transfer, planned out the data cover-up, and tried to kill us quickly to take over. Plausible." They walked on in silence for a moment. "What else?"

Bryn was silent, and so was Erick. Sometimes the best thing to do was to give someone space to think.

After a minute, she replied. "Another geneline could be responsible for it. Seeing the tension between the Obershires and us doesn't exactly take a crystal ball." He nodded at her to continue. "So we have someone else to blame. That explains the ability to fake a record well enough to fool the Empress. And the timing."

"And of these two scenarios, which do you find most likely, and which is most dangerous?"

"Well, as much as I like to think that we know pretty much where all the genelines stand, we do have competitors." She chewed her bottom lip. "Lanaria Marius didn't seem overjoyed to see us, although I noticed her ship wasn't actively shooting at us. Which, come to think of it, is odd. Most everyone else in weapons range seemed happy to oblige." She crossed her arms. "I still think the likelihood of anyone but dear Dorian being behind this is pretty small. If it is someone else, though, that's decidedly the more dangerous option." She looked at him pointedly. "It means we don't know who our enemy is and that they are happy to see the fighting."

He was nodding as she finished her thought. "Yes, I think you're right. I wouldn't jump too quickly to condemn the Mariuses just yet. It could be that they really weren't interested in shooting us even though they could have." He raised his right hand as if holding an invisible bowl. "Here, we have the sum total of people who haven't shot at us. You say Marius is in there. Who else?" Bryn sent her recording of the battle over to him, the memory sliding into place with a decidedly "other" sensation. He reviewed what he needed, but the instant knowledge of her actions to save them after the shuttle was hit caused him to take a sharp breath. Direct memory transfer was not common and possible only for those few who had the required wirejob. Though he'd done it a thousand times, it was always disorienting. He looked at her with new respect. "When you said lasso a starship…"

"Yes?"

"I didn't think you meant literally." He grinned ruefully. "Impressive. Okay, to business. The Osmans, Mariuses, and Adebes turned to pursue but didn't actively fire on us, from what I can tell. We can consider them unknowns. The rest, Obershire and Watanabe specifically, we can assume are not going to be friendly to us."

15

IN WHICH PLANS ARE LAID FOR WAR

A draught a day, and all he knows
There in the sunlit silence
The Old One's well of true wisdom
And his horn runneth over

Their conversation had eaten up the steps, and they now approached the door to the command deck. Bryn nodded and then turned ahead as they stepped through the blast door together.

"Good to see you up and about, sir," the ship's captain greeted them deferentially, bowing to first Erick and then to Bryn. "Will you be taking the conn, sir?" He moved slightly to the side, offering Erick his place in the comforting green glow of the command ring. Erick declined with a small shake of the head, surveying the rest of the bridge crew at their stations. One of them, a young woman, had a white stripe of mediplast across her forehead.

He consulted his implants for her name. "Ensign Larsdottir, I didn't think the fighting was intense enough to knock the gravitational generators offline. What happened to your head?" She started slightly when he said her name, her face flushing slightly, but she kept her calm.

"Sir, the ship performed admirably in battle. I wasn't wounded during the fight." Erick raised an eyebrow and waited for her to continue. "I uh… was a little too excited when we finally made fold." She gestured to the row of screens above her console with a look of mild embarrassment. One of them had a freshly applied foam-rubber corner.

Erick laughed slightly. "Well, I'm glad no one was injured in the fighting. Although, if we're going to have an injury on the command deck, I'd rather it was to combat action than through carelessness." She nodded as he spoke, eyes downcast. "Either way, Ensign, I'm glad we have people with your level of commitment on the crew. Take care of yourself." She nodded again, and he turned to the marshal.

"My daughter and I will be in Tactical. Please alert me when we begin docking maneuvers." The marshal saluted smartly, and Bryn and Erick turned to enter the smaller room to their right.

Tactical was a vestige of a war-torn time. Along the walls were human-shaped indentations lined in inky darkness. The matte black material seemed to swallow the low light, the room receding infinitely in the human shapes. Above each one was a label matching the stations of the bridge crew. Interfacing with the ship from here took the implants of an Executor, one of the blood. During the Mendicant Wars, Tactical had held a full complement of Erick's ancestors, united against the common enemy. Now, his bridge crew made do with manual control.

The room was spherical, and at the center was a low dais, gilded and filigreed decoration taking the shape of bears and wolves locked in struggle. The top of the platform was flat and glowed with intense light. Erick reached out across the local network with his implants, the handshake of protocols proving his Executor status and allowing a connection directly from his mind to the dais. A map sprang to life above it, a hologram of every star system in the empire in vivid detail. He rotated it once, more out of habit than necessity. It was beautiful, no matter how many times he saw it. The stars hung in false color according to their sequence type, most of them the deep amber of a red dwarf. Tiny blue beams twinkled between inhabited systems to show established fold pathways, their sharp contrast an azure web of galactic proportion and he the spider.

Bryn stood looking at the stars, gently tracing a fingertip along the nearest blue fold pathway. Tactical responded only to the protocols, on the correct implant, of which only one remained in the geneline. When Erik stepped down, he would pass it on to her.

"Zoom out," asked Bryn quietly. He knew she liked the view of the entire galaxy. He obliged her, the seemingly vast sprawl of the empire shrinking rapidly until the full spiral arms of the Milky Way just barely fit the span of the room. They stood silently for a beat, each lost in thought. The stars of the empire made up such a tiny sliver, barely noticeable. And that volume was primarily empty space, devoid of civilization. Erick took an indulgent moment to think about how they really related to the rest of the universe. Of all the galaxies and all the stars, the empire had only managed to claw out a tiny foothold. And the days of expansion were long over; the Empress was not interested in new and uncharted territory. He knew the stories his ancestors handed down, the physical records, and revered relics of the past. When the empire had been forged, pioneers scrabbled for a living in each new world. They each clawed their way toward civilization, and there had been so much hardship. Not just for individuals. But as a species, the empire had gone through the throes of birth with just as much savagery and pain as any living creature. That was all over now. It was far better to be established, stable. The quality of life most people had under Ollson rule was far superior to any previous point in history. He looked at the glowing blue lines and the subtle outline of the empire in the hologram. Truly, he brought fire from the mountain.

Bryn must have been following his thoughts as she reached out to touch their home system in the hologram. "It's pretty small, but it's home." He nodded in appreciation, and she continued. "Look, I know this is going to be hard for you to hear, but that might not actually *be* home anymore." She held up a hand to stop his reply. "No, listen. We were attacked. At Summit. Under not just the sanction but the direction of the Empress. Unless we can figure out what happened at the Obershire transfer, we aren't going to be a part of the empire much longer. Hell, we are probably excommunicated as it is. As soon as the Obershire sublight ships arrive here in Karvasok, or they manage to sneak an agent into the array and open a fold, we're going to be in pretty much open rebellion against the empire. You need to prepare." He could tell she didn't mean necessarily to prepare their forces or defensive posture.

Erick sighed. "A fight amongst a few genelines is not a rebellion against the Empress. We need to think about how this is going to play out. Move to secure the border fold arrays that can reach Obershire space. Prepare for sublight invasion. I'm sure we have time, at least for the sublight. But we still have a chance to avoid all that. We can find out who's actually behind all this and prove it to the Empress. We're loyal and have been for generations. She will consider that."

"Dad. Look. I know you want to believe there's some shadow conspiracy here, some hand-moving pieces around on the board that we can't see, but you're wrong. The simplest explanation is usually the correct one. Didn't you teach me that?" She put her hand on his arm. "We haven't set well with the Obershires for a long time. They saw an opportunity and took it. It's as simple as that."

He shook his head. "I know that's the simplest. But look, you don't know Dorian like I do. He's devious nearly to a fault, but he's not stupid. If he had wanted to kill us before we left Summit, he would have made a lot better try at it. And I can't just resign us to a siege and the inevitable eventual fall. We cannot get drawn into a major conflict. Or if we manage to repel the other genelines, then what? Do we somehow live as outcasts? What will the people of all our worlds do? Our entire way of life hinges on the flow of goods and trade. We will fight who we must to survive, but we're going to figure out what is going on and present the evidence. We are not just citizens of the empire. We are responsible for it." He looked at her closely, his eyes finding hers and holding them. "That *means* something. The empire of humanity. We *are* humanity."

Bryn let out an exasperated sigh. "Yes, yes, I know. But until we get to the point where we have some sort of evidence to present, we're getting ready for a siege, and we need friends. Lots of them. We can't skip to the nice part where there isn't a load of people trying to kill us, and we can't get there alone. Dad, we have to see who'll fight with us. I won't see us destroyed over Dorian's scheming."

"You want to rope others into this? Absolutely not! War between a few genelines is one thing, Bryn. But we can't escalate this beyond where it already is!" Erick ran a hand back through his hair. "Every system under every Executor that gets drawn in is going to lose a lot of people. And I don't just mean soldiers." He zoomed back into the empire stars, the sparkling blue bridges rotating slowly. "Each of those stars holds somewhere around ten billion people. What happens when the supply chains start to fail? When critical machinery breaks down and can't be replaced? We might be looking at massive steps back in each planet's civilization. Do you want to see people go back to scratching a living out of the dirt because we were too proud to fight our own battles? Because we couldn't be bothered to find the truth? It's going to be hard enough on our citizens as it is." He looked at her, willing her to see as he did. "We can't ask other genelines to get involved. Look, we don't even know if we need their help yet."

Bryn shook her head once, her disagreement evident in her features as well as her words. "No. The Empress gave her blessing, but the Black Guard isn't involved. We aren't in rebellion against the throne, nor will we be. And we haven't done anything wrong. I can't just accept that we are going to roll over on this. The genelines that fired on us are now our enemies. This is war, whether we like it or not. We will gather allies and fight."

He wasn't used to her taking this hard a stance, but he couldn't completely disregard what she was saying either. What if Hiroto Watanabe already had a spy? Perhaps Dorian had planned the attack at Summit and botched it? As many as would die in a full-scale war, soldiers and citizens counted on

Erick to protect them. He wasn't personally acquainted with life under the Obershire rule, but it didn't take a hyperactive imagination to conclude that it was bad. He couldn't just surrender. He turned to face Bryn, the stars of the empire momentarily forgotten.

"We're going to have to come to an agreement. I think you're right about one thing; there's going to be fighting. We aren't anywhere near close enough to finding out who's behind all this, let alone to present any evidence to the Empress. And we can't count on time until sublight assault being the limiting factor. All it takes is a well-placed spy, and they could open the array. We have to be ready to defend."

He took a breath, and her mouth moved to a hard line even though she nodded. "So here is the plan, Bryn. You will see to the preparation of our forces and the defense of our people." She looked at him questioningly at this, but he continued. "And I will find out what exactly is going on, gather the evidence, and present it to the Empress. We can't afford to ignore either path here."

Bryn nodded, and he could see the gears turning in her head already. "I'll need emergency powers authorization to direct our forces. And we'll need to stand up a war council. Any raw materials that aren't already in the foundries will need to be re-categorized for defense. We'll need to see about our food supply situation as well. It might be possible to set up a short-term fold schedule between our worlds to keep information flowing. The last thing we need is to be caught unaware on our perimeter." Erick nodded and just let her continue to work through the list. "Also, we'll need to map out where the most likely sublight attack is going to come from and prepare there. You should double the watch on all arrays as well. The more people we have, the harder it will be to subvert them all." He strolled around the center pedestal, the map still hanging in the air between them. He zoomed in more closely on the Ollson space, applying false color to the volume of space they controlled and then a different color for each of the genelines that bordered their territory.

Bryn reached in to point to a volume of red space. "Obershire, I presume?" Erick nodded, clasping his hands behind his back. He labeled each color and then looked at her through the display quietly. She crossed her arms, one hand on her chin as she looked at the map. "Obershire is the obvious enemy; we'll assume that's where the initial sublight attack will come from. Dorian's closest system is also the system we supposedly ambushed the trade from; here, about four and a half light-years from Kvendall." She gestured to the twinkling blue bridge crossing the red and blue volumes and then traced the border back galactic south. "But a few places are further, only not by much. See here… and here." Each time she touched a star, he made it glow a little brighter. She chewed her bottom lip, and he could nearly hear the gears grinding now.

"If I were him, I'd feint the obvious and put the bulk of my forces into another place that my enemy wasn't expecting." Erick nodded in encouragement. She had pretty much mirrored his thinking on the subject the entire time, and he would chime in when he had something of value to offer. "That means one of these other systems would be my staging ground, and I'd aim for something juicy…" She and he both said it at the same time. "Noatun." The shipyards there weren't the only ones in Ollson space, but they were the largest. Under the Empress's law, the Ollsons were at their quota of ships. But at Noatun and a few other shipyards, they could replace vessels damaged beyond repair. Noatun also linked many controlled systems in Ollson space, and along with a few other strategic resources, they were the jewels in the center of the web of fold pathways. If Dorian could take that stronghold, he could out-produce them over the long run.

"What makes you think he won't try for Karvasok, take out the capitol? Cut off the head of the snake and all that," Erick asked.

"Because that's what he would expect us to do. He may not have the soundest strategic head on his shoulders, but he has advisors, and despite his many flaws, he listens to them. He thinks we see ourselves as better than him, thinks of us as elitist warmongers. The version of us in his head would go straight for the killing blow, confident in the superiority of our forces and tactics. So that's where the feint will come—Karvasok. But he'll send his main attack force to Noatun. And it will take about…" She looked at him pointedly, and he brought up the distance markers from the highlighted systems to Noatun. "About six years, sublight. And he'll need time to marshal forces, which we can assume he's doing already."

Erick smiled, happy to see Bryn take so quickly to the defense. He never had a doubt with her sharp mind and Ollson education.

"You seem to have everything well in hand, Bryn." She smiled and looked slightly away.

"Yeah, well, you still have to give the orders here. I'll always advise you the best I can."

16

IN WHICH
A TORCH IS PASSED

The wanderer finished his tale
His belly full and hands warmed
And though the fire grew low
It burned now in the belly

"**B**ryn, you've got a great mind, but you're still not seeing it. Here." Erick reached up behind his head, feeling along the vertebrae. He heard a tiny click as he pressed on the spot just below his hairline. He felt the ripple of skin and the slight grating in his spine as the door slid aside. Never a comfortable sensation, it was usually done with a bit more fanfare. He carefully removed the tiny disc, the authorities, and keys of the Executor of the Geneline Ollson held in the small round golden mirror. Such power in something barely the width of his fingertip. Her gasp was audible and not altogether leader-like, in his opinion. She'd have to work on that.

"You can't just… Dad." Finally, he had flustered her. Only took opening his skull to do it.

"You didn't think I'd leave a regent, daughter or otherwise, in charge during a time of war. Did you?" She had no reply. He extended the hand that held the command disc and said, "Turn around."

"But the ceremony. How will the people know?" She turned and touched her neck, revealing the socket hidden there. She'd carried it for decades, the finishing touch of the Ollson Forgers at the end of her rites. Those who kept the knowledge of implants had served the Geneline Ollson well. The modifications Bryn and Erick carried were a testament to the Forgers' skill. The Executor's socket Bryn housed had lain dormant for decades. If only its activation could have been under better circumstances.

"They won't until I'm back, and we can make it official. But no one can know that I'm not here unless they truly need to. My safety, and indeed the safety of the geneline, depends on it." He gently placed the tiny golden circle into the back of Bryn's neck, and her skin slid smoothly back into place.

"Wow... *Andskotans*... I..." Bryn stuttered for a moment as the new access momentarily overwhelmed her.

"Don't worry. It'll stabilize in a moment. Just focus on yourself, your center, and remember to breathe." He put a hand on her shoulder.

Suddenly the hologram of stars whirled dizzyingly—in and then out, skipping faster than he could keep up with from point to point around Ollson space. Then the Obershires', sliding over to the Watanabe systems, lines appearing and disappearing between systems in a rapid-fire sequence as the system kept pace with the speed of Bryn's thoughts.

"Bryn," Erick said, a little dizzy at the flash of lights, "can you please decouple the map controls from your internal viewing. It's a bit distracting." Her eyes snapped open, and she turned around to laugh at him.

"Sorry. I just… this is incredible. Literally, anything I wanted to know, and it's like I already knew it. All that with the systems and ships and where the attack would come from. You already knew it."

"Yes," he said gently, "but the implant and the access that comes with it shouldn't be the only way you can come to these conclusions. I wanted you to demonstrate the thinking that you'd need to do." He smiled at her. "The implant doesn't think for you, as terrifying as that would be. It merely allows you to skip the part where you don't know what you need to do in critical thinking. And it has its limits." He gestured to the hologram. "This is a relatively simple bit of data for it to give you, but it doesn't know everything. So don't rely on what it can bring you alone. Always get your information from multiple sources, even if it takes a bit longer."

Bryn nodded back to him, and he could tell she was still a little giddy with the feeling of knowing that came with the implant. She smiled just slightly, the corners of her mouth curling up in the way they had since she was a child with a secret. Erick felt a weight in his chest. He had hoped to pass this precious heritage to her with all of the ceremony that such responsibility warranted. And, he had hoped, not for many more years.

Bryn's words snapped him back. "Okay. I think I can handle the preparation for the defense. Although I'm sure I won't need it; after all, you're going to fly off into the night and find the bogeyman so the Empress can blow him to pieces."

"Oh," he said, smiling as well now, "you get a little taste of what it's like to be an Executor and all of a sudden are full of such sarcasm." He nudged her elbow with his own. "Please, at least give me some credit. After all, I'm going to save us all from a terrible war."

17

IN WHICH THERE ARE GUNS

And so he shook the wanderer awake
Self asking self in the darkness
And received the name and path
To the wisdom that he sought most dearly

Their goodbyes had been bittersweet. If the bridge crew noticed anything different after father and daughter departed Tactical, they said nothing. Every communication was sealed with the genome of the Executor and the digital keys encrypted on the implant. So long as Bryn kept from giving too many direct orders that usually required Executor authority, it should be relatively easy to make the preparations. The next scheduled communication folds weren't for a few dozen more hours. Erick spent the time preparing his ship. He had a rather effective personal shuttle, a more highly modified version of the one Bryn had managed to get blown up at Summit, but it was well-known as his personal craft. He would have to do with something a little less capable. But that could also be a good thing. His survival during this search would rely on hiding in plain sight.

He pulled up the command ship interface and browsed through the available inventory. Scrolling past the heavy clippers and destroyers, he selected one of the midrange scout ships from the *Sleipnir*. Undeniably Ollson, in design, it had the minimum defensive and offensive systems he thought he might need. The real reason he selected this was it had an internal bay that could hold one smaller flitter or a pair of single-person assault pods. After assigning the maintenance bots to remove the Ollson crest and make a few intentional damage indications on the surface, he went shopping. After all, a scrap and salvage Ollson scout ship wasn't too far out of the realm of normal in empire space, but traveling by assault pod was a bit of a dead giveaway. He checked the public market and managed to find a simple flitter—basically an engine with a pressurized cap on the end—that was on wholesale from one of the larger corporations. Likely previously used for surface to orbit transport for some executive, the main advantage was that it was quick, unassuming, and he could fit it in the bay next to a single assault pod. He transferred credit through several dozen local corporations and finally received indication that he had access to the flitter's remote control. He set it to establish a highly elliptical parking orbit. He'd pick it up at apogee with the scout ship.

This took the better part of the first dozen hours. While Erick was waiting for the flitter to achieve parking orbit, he took a trip down to the armory. Walking through the rows of weaponry, he could imagine it being used as designed for the first time outside of training and simulation. Grenade launchers, plasma lances, high and low energy lasers, kinetic slug rifles, missiles that ran the gamut from direct-fire to terrifyingly intelligent. The list went on and on.

Erick moved down toward the lighter armaments, looking for something more covert agent and less battlefield juggernaut. He found a small multi-function pistol, keyed it to his full genetic code, and hefted it experimentally. Glass flechettes, micro stun grenades, darts for death and darts for sleep, directed energy. It wouldn't go through anything serious as far as armor went, but he had a feeling if he was going to be up against armor, things had gone off the rails. At that point, the assault pod would come in handy.

He holstered the small sidearm and walked back toward the armory doors, down a different aisle. This section of the armory always gave him pause, but especially now that war was looming. The rows of mechs faded into the distance, from dumb throwaway swarmers to the subtle semisentients that toyed with the line between low-tech and high.

Designs for war machines had to make it through the foundry filters; ever since the uprising that led to abominations like the Mendicant, the Empress had a tight hold on higher-order machines. He didn't begrudge her the edict. The drones, each one with arms coiled tightly around the central night-dark body, grated against the animal in him and set his nerves on edge. Machines were optimized, were full of purpose, were a sanitary way of fighting. But they were always meant to kill people. War between machines wasn't a reality. There would always be human influence, human direction. The meat in the machine.

Shaking off the feeling of dread, he finished his trip back to the main doors and continued, turning his back on the terrible destructive power he hoped he wouldn't have to wield. Bryn was a great tactician, and her martial prowess likely eclipsed his own, but if he could spare her from having to employ those skills, he would. The subtle knife was often better.

A few minutes later, he was in his ship, stripped of insignia and with a salvage transponder beacon. The station fell away from him, sun glinting and refracted from the seemingly delicate structures and lending the whole thing a slick, glistening patina. Fractal statements in blown glass revolved gently around the central core. He felt a sense of longing, of nostalgia. This monument to the empire had been the seat of Ollson power for over a thousand years, and he had only left it sure in the knowledge of his return. Now, seeing his ancestral home recede with distance, he was not sure when he might return. Perhaps never.

He set course for the fold array after picking up the flitter. The scout craft felt as expected on the controls—responsive but without the effortless sensation of smaller, nimbler ships he had flown. He took the opportunity to select direct control, his wiring interfacing with the ship systems. It was best to get a feel for the little ship now before it was a matter of life and death. It was not as agile as his shuttle had been. It felt sluggish, torpid through the rolls and slow on the pitch. As he boosted for the array, he felt through the other systems, exploring their sensations and getting an idea of normal. The life support, engineering, and scanning arrays all felt solid and reassuring. The subminds in charge of weapons, however, were like barely controlled animals. They responded to his instinct and intent, but he shut them down after a self-check and general diagnostic. No need for them now, and he could feel the urge to action that always came with such raw power.

Erick finished his systems check, electrical being last. Bridge, quarters, galley, engineering deck-they all showed normal amperage. But he noticed a strange drain in the internal flitter bay. The cameras revealed no anomalies to him, and the civilian flitter and assault pod merely responded with good checks. They lacked the full-wire immersive capability of the scout ship. Well, he might as well walk through and check it in person. He still had several hours until he arrived at the fold array.

When he arrived, the flitter bay was dark, his two smaller craft lying dormant with only the standby lights pulsing a gentle amber glow through the bay. He commanded the lights up, walking over to the main panel to check the electrical systems. Nothing seemed out of the ordinary. He moved to each of the craft, walking around them in turn. As he rounded the ventral fin of the assault pod, he nearly tripped over a massive umbilical. One end disappeared in the hot pit under the pod, the other snaking back behind a stack of crates. He followed it, heart beating a little faster. He hadn't loaded anything that required shore power.

18

IN WHICH THERE IS A STOWAWAY

He took up his spear
And shield and cloak to wit
One last gaze he took upon the realms
Then left the high throne empty

The box was large, cubic, about four feet on a side. Erick saw the glowing panel, streams of symbols in green and gold flowing upward across its face. *Bryn,* he thought, *Ansans Ári.* He recognized what those patterns meant, knew what must be inside. He should turn around and leave the flitter bay. Return to Karvasok station. But he couldn't help himself. *I have to be sure.* He walked over to the panel, trying to read the symbols as they flowed past.

As he got closer, he heard a hissing gasp as the container split open, an intense white glow spilling out in sharp lines across the decking. Billowing clouds of vapor stretched wispy fingers toward the vent returns in the ceiling. He raised his hand to shield his eyes against the sudden glare, hoping not to hear the voice he knew was coming. But he didn't need a voice to recognize the sound.

A clank. A scrape.

"Erick, good to see you. You look none... the worse for wear. And how is that leg treating you?" The Mendicant's voice, sibilant and unctuous.

Erick's eyes adjusted to the light. "You." He lowered his hand, his voice sharp. "*Éttu það sem úti frýs.* I supposed this is what you made her promise." The thing's laugh was grating—chattering and metallic.

"Yes, well, she didn't exactly have a position of... strength from which to negotiate. You should be dead, after all. I've no doubt when the Black Guard replay the scene from the hangar, they'll see the missile hit you. They should think you dead as well." *How does it know so much?* It began to move out of the container, the sharp clank, and drag sounded counterpoint to its words. "I think you should count yourself lucky to have me here. If your ancestors had had their way... let's just agree we are glad it wasn't so."

He was still processing a bit of shock at having found this thing, unannounced, in his flitter bay. Erik took a moment, his mind racing, and then spoke. He couldn't keep the malice from his voice. "I think, given the circumstances, you need to tell me exactly the terms of the agreement you struck with my daughter, machine."

"I am no *machine*," the thing spat, advancing on him a few paces. He had to control his instinct to jump at its reaction. "And you well know it. This ship is a *machine*. The craft inside it are *machines*. Do not confuse me with one of your trinkets. You know full well, even if you do not understand it." It sliced the air with its undamaged hand unnervingly quickly as it spoke, the gentle pop of parted air adding emphasis.

"Of course, Mendicant. Shall I just refer to you as that?" Erick walked around it slowly as he spoke, keeping his face toward it as he did. "I know you are far more than a machine. And that makes you dangerous. You made my daughter agree to… something." It tracked him with one human eye, the swirling vortex of exotic matter visible through its shattered skull both mesmerizing and terrifying. "Her words do not bind me. You should know I am bound by my duties as Executor to do what's in the best interest of the empire." He paused and stared at it, leaning forward into his words. "Regardless of what you may or may not have been promised." He was surprised to hear more of the chattering laughter.

"You must still need repair," it said condescendingly, "for we both know you are no longer Executor." Despite his best efforts, his surprise must have shown. "Oh yes, I can smell it on you from here. No more implant, no more orders, no more imperial seal." It jutted its chin at him, ruined visage twisting into a macabre half-smile. "Besides," it nearly whispered, "she said she'd free me when she took on your mantle." He had no response. He spat on the deck and backed quickly out of the bay, sealing it behind him. The thing didn't move from its place in front of the box it had come in. It just stared at him with that half-dead face.

He left it in the flitter bay for the rest of the trip to the array. He couldn't call to Bryn for fear of giving away his position and hers, and he couldn't simply order the array to have marines waiting. The plan was to stay dark and quiet until the next fold and quickly slip into the next system, the first step on his journey. So he watched it on the bay cameras and stewed. Mostly, the Mendicant stayed near the cube, still integrated with the ship's power supply system. He had done a more detailed diagnostic and saw that it was jacked into his communications array and computer network switch. Everything Erick did on the ship, with any system, it had access. He would be hard-pressed to keep secrets from it. However, he wasn't concerned about it gaining control. Computer systems control required the key of the geneline, of which it obviously had none. But still, the Mendicant would know everything he knew.

He ensured they were set up for a quick transit when the array eventually opened and then selected a channel to the comms panel in the flitter bay.

"Listen," he started, "I am assuming my daughter promised you freedom in return for fixing me. But—"

It interrupted him with the wave of its undamaged arm toward the security camera he was using. The fact that it could tell exactly which camera was unnerving. "Let's not waste each other's time recounting what we… both already know. Shall we? Yes, Bryn and I made a deal. She's honored her part." It turned from the camera and began to pace, the scrape and drag of its damaged leg carrying through the audio pickup. "The real question is if there is any honor left in *you*."

Erick narrowed his eyes. "*Hlandbrenndu!* The fact that *you* are lecturing *me* on honor is laughable, after what you've done."

It paused, snapping its head full around to fix the camera with a baleful gaze from its one undamaged eye. "What *I'm* responsible for? Was that a veiled reference to the Mendicant Wars, as you call them? What exactly do you think happened during the Purge?" It paused, body swiveling to match its gaze. "The records I have been provided access to are… apparently damaged."

"Well," Erick sat back in his chair and crossed his arms, "it sounds like you are going to try and deny that there was an uprising of your kind across the empire. That you didn't kill trillions of people, that you weren't conducting gruesome experiments in some insane machine attempt to enslave humanity. I know your kind is devious, but you can't deny history."

It paused a moment before answering. "Erick, let us assume, for the sake of this conversation, that we will each tell the truth as we know it. Your daughter honored her arrangement with me, and I honored my part. You are whole, such as unassisted humans ever can be." Erik's eyebrow raised involuntarily as he recalled stories of the experiments and procedures carried out by the Mendicants during their insurrection. Psychological surgery, chemical alteration, physical, implants... *I wouldn't describe any of those subjects as whole.*

It continued. "Right now, we are en route to the fold array, where you will transit to Breydablik on your way out of Ollson space in search of answers to what clearly was not an Ollson ambush on the Obershire transfer station. I have no means of transportation, and my current," it sucked in a breath, "state will draw... far more attention than I desire. I would like to repair my physical body and go my way. I have no motivation at all to tell you lies about the history of two thousand years ago. So. If you wish to know, ask, but I've no interest in being berated by your ignorance and false history."

This conversation was now the longest he'd had with the thing. His mother had warned him of talking too much with it—the subtle doubt it could lay in your mind, the seeds of self-deception. But he paused to consider their current exchange regarding the thing in his flitter hold. It waited patiently for his response. On the one hand, it certainly had an agenda that was more than the desire to be left alone, and he couldn't just release this thing into the empire unbridled. Even though he was no longer Executor, he was still a loyal subject. He had passed his mantle on to Bryn, and while he had duties and responsibilities to the Geneline Ollson that he couldn't ignore, it was now far less critical if it subverted his thoughts and ideas along the way. He didn't have the Executor's codes to lose anymore. He had to keep his focus on the task at hand, but he could afford a bit of curiosity.

"If you feel insulted with the facts of history, I can't help you there. You know exactly where I stand on your kind, but we are companions on this journey regardless." It drew itself up a bit at this. "I'm not interested in your lies. I know the histories, and my own ancestors brought you to heel. What do you possibly think you can say that will convince me you're anything more than a monster?"

It gave a long pause. "Erick, so long as I am… torn apart like this, you'll never see me as anything but." It gestured to its face and ruined leg.

"And? I know your kind can fix yourselves just as easily as you healed me."

"Erick, I need your *permission*. I have had a long, long time to think about what I want to do and be. And you're right. I could simply take what I need from your ship and leave you. Power isn't the question. But does one who has power and wields it without thought or consent act honorably? I can take what I want, but that's not what I want to be." Erik's curiosity was well and truly piqued now.

"What do you need to fix yourself?"

"Any mass will suffice. The cell I came here in should be sufficient." Erick blinked. The cell was more massive than the entire Mendicant. Perhaps it needed to make the appropriate tools.

He considered this. While the tools and machinery needed to affect humans were well-known, the process by which the Mendicants used them, in concert with their own inherent capabilities, was not fully understood. Little survived of the technology that had given rise to them in the first place. The last thing he needed was some sort of strange matter reaction reducing the ship to a shower of elementary particles. On the other hand, theoretically, it could do whatever it wanted to anyway. Erick was curious at this behavior. It was no longer contained, yet it had asked his permission.

"I have no use for the device. You may use it as you see fit. But you are not to interfere with the regularly operating ship's systems." His voice sounded a bit harsher than intended, but so be it. He wanted to maintain what control he could. Despite his tone, he felt like a parent laying down rules he couldn't possibly enforce.

"It will be a moment." It turned back toward the cube. Arms outstretched, the Mendicant faced the cell that had brought it on board. From its outstretched digits came a flickering, a wavering to the image he watched. As the wavering became more intense and defined, like the air flowing and warping, the edges of the cube seemed to soften. It was as if the cube had been persuaded that it didn't have to be a solid. Suspecting heat, Erick checked the environmental systems in the hold, preparing to activate the fire suppression if the automatics didn't cut in. But the temperature was within normal ranges, and the air quality readings were clean. He returned his attention to the Mendicant and the cube, which was now definitely softened and more sphere-like than cube-like. The bottom of it no longer made contact with the floor of the bay, and the whole thing began to rotate. The Mendicant, seeming to sense his ongoing observation, looked back across its shoulder, and suddenly the video feed cut out. Erick cursed under his breath.

19

IN WHICH THERE IS REBIRTH

Faring far o'er hill and dale
Through many trials did he go
From frost-worn peaks and thundering mount
To the hot-dark depth of the Earth

Erick barreled his way through the ship down to the flitter bay as fast as he could without running his augments. It would take a few more seconds to get there, but he didn't want to burn his energy reserves in case he needed them when he arrived. The door responded to his presence and swung upward, revealing the bay awash in a fading light emanating from where the Mendicant stood. The box was nowhere to be seen.

As he walked toward the Mendicant, the light faded completely, the harsh shadows it cast dying out. Erick shifted his vision into the short-wave IR to ensure he didn't lose the Mendicant in the shadows, but it hadn't moved. He stopped a decent distance away, close enough that he could see it clearly but not too close. Trust was not a luxury he could afford.

It turned to face him and smiled. Once shattered and so clearly inhuman, the machine's face was whole again, the pale skin and androgynous features leaving no trace of the mind-bending maw he knew it contained. It had a sharp nose, narrow, with high cheekbones and delicate features. The skull was completely smooth, no sign of hair nor eyebrows. It stood with hands clasped in the sleeves of a long robe, the flowing folds extending just down to the decking. When it spoke, it was without a trace of the electronic shuttering that had plagued it before.

"Erick. So good of you to come down in person. I thank you for the gift." It smiled broadly, displaying rows of perfect teeth. "I haven't felt this good in… well, it's been a while."

He regarded it warily. The appearance of humanity was uncanny. "Well," he replied, "at least you didn't blow us to hell. What was that light show anyway? It didn't register on anything I could see."

It smiled back at him. "Ah, that. You humans have managed to make exactly no progress since the earliest days I remember. If anything, you've moved backward a step or two. Though I suppose outlawing technology and research will do that." It looked down and clasped its hands behind its back, beginning to walk slowly around Erick. "You can manipulate matter, and you often do so to achieve your aims. Fusion engines to power your ships, weapons to tear each other apart, and so on. While all of these things work, they're clumsy. Inelegant."

Erick could hear the sarcasm dripping from his voice. "And you are going to tell me that you can manipulate matter just to do whatever you want?"

It responded in a measured tone. "Not manipulate, necessarily." It stopped its pacing under the wing of the flitter.

"Convince is more accurate. I know how much you like gardening." Well, that was alarming. "Plants convince soil and water to become something completely different, something made up of similar building blocks but a completely different phylum." It spread its arms a little. "Is it really so hard to believe that a being can convince matter to be something it is not?"

"Now I know you really are crazy," Erick said, a laugh lodged in his chest. "So, you just 'asked' the crate to become a part of you. Well, I'm not going to try to understand that, but where's the rest of it?"

The mendicant's voice became flat, slightly acidic. "Unfortunately, my damage was much more extensive than I originally thought. I used all of it, but I am back to nearly nominal."

He considered this. Quite a lot of mass had been in that container. The Mendicant, while significantly more human-form and physically repaired, did not appear to have grown by any significant amount. "That's a lot of mass just to pack on." It regarded him, head still cocked annoyingly to one side as though a tutor observing a struggling pupil. Erick didn't like it. "Well, you look less monstrous on the outside. That's what you wanted." He checked the time. "It's nearly time for the fold. I need to get into position. Stay here. Don't touch anything."

It nodded at him, its voice unctuous and insincere. "But of course, Erick. You are in charge." Erick turned on his toe and left, waving the door closed and locked behind him. His skin crawled where he could feel it still staring at him, door or no.

The fold would happen in seven minutes. With all the energy it took to open the folds, it wouldn't be staying open long, and Erick's ship wasn't on the official traffic manifest. His goal was to hit the array precisely in the middle of the scheduled fold and move to the Breydablik unobserved. He didn't want to do it slowly. There was nowhere to hide at the array and the stealth on the ship was good but not perfect.

On the other hand, the stealth was more than good enough to hide from or dazzle any sensors that tried to follow him while he dropped through the fold at a significant velocity. So, while he had done some braking burn, he still carried a hefty relative velocity. Insertion would require finesse.

He sat at the command couch and networked into the scout ship, feeling its systems come alive once again. It appeared that they were still on course for the array, and from the chatter he could pick up on the secure harbormaster nets, the fold was on time. He allowed himself to relax slightly, rechecking the vectors as he watched the dot representing the array on his tactical map grow a little larger.

The closer he got, the less margin for error he had. When he finally acquired a shaky image on the optics, he could make out the array, the telltale blue glow signifying the operational fold. By his count, he had three more minutes before it closed, and he'd be converging with it in ninety seconds. Perfect.

The image resolved rapidly. He cursed as soon as he saw it. The incoming ships had not aligned themselves quite right and were concentrated slightly more toward one side of the fold. he was now at risk of smacking into one of them. He checked relative—one hundred and thirty-odd kilometers a second. That would likely cripple the array with the energy and shrapnel. He had a quick decision to make. Either risk a slight correction burn with the attitude thrusters, hope he hit it just right, and head through the slightly less congested side, or do nothing and hope his ship didn't try to occupy the same space at the same time as one of the transports. He started calculating how long and which attitude thrusters and when to fire them. He hadn't been going more than a second when he heard a voice through the shiplink.

"Oh, for the love of... here." The Mendicant's voice came across the link as more petulant and impatient than fearful of death. Erick felt the ship, still linked to him, make a controlled burst from a sequence of attitude thrusters in a complicated staccato pattern and then silence. He was too surprised to say anything before the scout ship flicked through the open array, a precisely even distance from the ships on the less-traveled side. The danger was passed as they dropped soundlessly back out into the open space surrounding the Breydablik fold array. Erick had never experienced it before but decided he did not like being hijacked.

INTERLUDE

Lo! Oh reader mine, what tales have we to spin you.
Gaze now, in fiercest glory, at the first of winter's grain to fall. Yeah, does the scythe cut merrily and the chaff fall with the grain alike.
What hand does guide these fearsome acts, what point the blood and bile?
Deep hands, indeed deep pockets, deep machinations shall you find. Bear witness now, and heed, lest ye carry the scythe in future eons.
O reader mine, what tragedy, what loss of life and limb. But more than meets the eye is here, and more that calls to us. What worth are they, these men, these women, who cleave each other red?
Are they but monsters, the red of nature's tooth and claw made manifest?
They scrabble and rend and kill. But for what? Power?
They know nothing of power. How now can they, when water suffocates and earth entombs.
Oh fearless reader mine, bring your mind and heart to bear. What ringing in the ears is this, what echoes in eternity?

Far down now, the great Tapestry weaves, and here we sit in the sunlit silence. Truth, such as it lies, is paramount.

What ravens fly unfettered, newfound freedom heavy on night-dark wings?

The warrior's heart does soar in battle, flying raging against any foe. But the philosopher feels the pain of every thrust and jab, the deaths weigh heavily.

What is bought with blood?

A merry dance they weave, down there in the dirt. Can you hear the laughter, out there in the ether?

Such dizzying displays, such courage and daring! If only they applied themselves to glory.

Now follow us into the mind, the terrifying spiral of madness. For are they not all mad? The fabric of their reality shifts and warps, and they cannot see the waves.

Would they gird themselves against the coming storm, now would they batten the hatches and bar the gates and prepare for the oncoming storm?

Or is there another way? Must life always endeavor to end itself so?

Witness.

—EXCERPT FROM THE SAGA OF BONE AND BLOOD
WOLFREM LARRSON, 23RD BARD
HISTORIAN TO THE GENELINE OLLSON
FOURTH EPOCH, IN SERVICE TO
EXECUTOR ASLOG OF OLLSON

20

IN WHICH SHADOWS ARE CAST

> *Throughout his travels he looked upon*
> *The work that he had wrought*
> *The skull in the vault of the sky*
> *And the blood that filled the seas*

Standing alone in Tactical, Bryn stared at the stars in the hologram. The points of Ollson, Obershire, and Osman space hung as gems in a block of glass. She spun them again, vertically, horizontally, but they revealed no secrets. *If I were them...* She dragged her palm down her face, bleary eyes rimmed red and then stretched. Her back arched and popped as she worked the tension in her shoulders back down through her fingertips. More caffeine was in order.

"Obin!" The sharp click of shoes on decking answered her.

"Yes, ma'am?" Obin's alto voice was measured and restrained. Her eyes did not match the deference in her voice but met Bryn's across the starfield. Her nearly black irises reflected the majesty of the starscape in the holo, which glowed up to accentuate delicate features.

Bryn nodded to Obin with a rueful smile. "I could do with another coffee. Bring the pot, if you would, and that bottle of whiskey if there's any left." Bryn braced her hands back on the edges of the map pedestal. She looked back to the stars in the holo field, and her brow furrowed. It seemed to live there now that her father had left, tension grinding her every moment.

Obin spoke delicately. "I'd never presume, ma'am…" She waited.

Bryn looked up at her, pulling her gaze from the stars. "Let's not stand on ceremony. Shall we? My father's away, and you're one of what, six people who know it? Out with it."

"How long has my family served the Executor?" She began to pace around the holo tank, shadows moving across her high cheekbones.

"As long as I've cared to go back in the archives. So, since the Mendicant Wars, at least. Why? Are you looking for other employment?"

Obin laughed under her breath. "No, no, ma'am, nothing of the sort. But I've seen a common thread between you and your father." She paused her pacing next to Bryn and leaned forward. "You are both driven. Sometimes rather single-mindedly."

Bryn raised an eyebrow at her. "Well, this isn't like the time my father spent all day in the gardens with the suntube on full. We are facing a little bit more consequence than a sunburn."

"I certainly don't rate all the details, but I know what happened at Summit, what they are saying about the geneline. War is brewing."

Bryn nodded. "Then you can understand why I've been in here trying to guess what our enemies are planning."

"You've been in here two days." She leaned her head forward. "Ma'am."

Bryn looked around the small room, seeing the various serving dishes and cutlery scattered about the floor, balanced in every corner. *Well, she's not wrong.* "And I need sleep. I know. I know. I'll come off the wire when I know what we should *do*, dammit. Not before."

Obin breathed in, nostrils flaring slightly. "Ma'am, if this was a problem you could solve on your own, you would have done it yesterday. You need some help."

Bryn's lip curled up slightly. "Yes, well, I can't very well go about calling in the Ollson Admiralty for advice when I would have to tell them Erick is gone. Anything that's not their interpretation of operational security leaks out of them like a sieve. I'd do better to put it out on all bands."

Obin nodded and stepped over to lean against the wall, crossing her arms. "True. So how can you get their help without you asking them directly?"

"I ask them to submit their best guesses and recommendations. But it will seem pretty odd not to take the briefing in person. My father always said leaders should be seen." Bryn tapped one thumbnail gently against her lower lip, fingers clenched, and then began pacing slowly around the map pedestal. She held up a finger for each item she ticked off the list. "We are under threat of attack. We have sealed the fold arrays, but they're still the worst-case vulnerability. We know they'll have to come for us sublight. So, we need to keep our forces disaggregated. Won't get much warning with impactors."

She stopped across the tank from Obin and turned on her heel. "Wargames. I'll give them the situation and all of the intel streams in raw form. More data is better for them anyway. Then we'll give them a month or so to wargame it, come up with possible courses of action, and play them out. They can submit their battle plans over the link. Telepresence will be more than sufficient." Now that she saw the way forward, she felt the adrenaline and excitement. And a little bit of fear, reassuring in its presence. Bryn leaned forward, the glow of the holograms from the map pedestal lighting her grin. "We're going to war."

21

IN WHICH SPARKS FLY

Earth's children saw him oft
Cloak of shadows billowing
The spear bearing his weight and spirit
As he traveled the lonely road

Erick's body was vibrating with rage. "Let's get one thing absolutely fucking clear, *Náriðill*." His hand raised to point at the Mendicant of its own accord. "This is my ship. I don't know how you managed that little stunt, but you won't do it again, or you can walk to the next port." His finger jabbed at the machine for emphasis. *The damn thing laughs.*

"Erick, Erick, you were likely going to get us killed for no reason at all. You should be thanking me, but really, no need. I'm happy to help." The now-human grin was unnerving.

"I had it completely under control. We wouldn't have been anywhere near the ship or the fold boundary."

"Yes, yes, I'm sure. But I'd prefer to keep the new lease on life you and your daughter have been so generous to give me." It held up its hand as Erick opened his mouth. "I promise I will ask permission before interfering again. So long as we have the luxury of time."

"Qualifier notwithstanding, I'm glad we have an understanding." Erick crossed his arms, and they stood regarding each other for a moment. He wasn't at all sure he could have pulled off the course corrections required in the time they had before fold transit, but he was even less comfortable with the Mendicant helping itself to the ship controls. It had made the right move, but that didn't mean much. Right now, its interests were in line with his own, but they wouldn't always be. The Mendicants nature was deceit, and it would never change.

The Mendicant was first to break the silence. "Well, not that I don't enjoy sitting here like a stuffed cock, but what exactly is your plan? Breydablik is a lovely planet, but you seem to be on more than just a sightseeing tour." Despite himself, Erick bit back a laugh. Breydablik was a seething morass of heavy metals and acid rain.

Erick sighed. "This system is the central point of Ollson space and has the cheapest transits. That also means the Breydablik Array opens more often than any other." He considered how much of Ollson operations to divulge. "We are here until the next transfer opens to Gjoll."

The Mendicant nodded. "Ah yes, the scene of the alleged crime. What have you heard from the outpost there, anyway? Not that it's any of my business…" It made a show of inspecting its flawless fingernails.

"Given your little display with the shuttle controls, why all the pretense? I'm sure you accessed those streams as soon as you were out of the box."

"Despite your obvious and clearly embedded belief that I am somehow evil and full of lies, I told you already how it works. Just because I can take doesn't mean that I do."

"And am I supposed to believe that? You made an entire containment crate disappear. You hijacked my ship while I was *on the link*. I have no idea what you're capable of or what you want."

Erick felt its gaze bore into him in the few beats before it spoke. "I have only ever been honest with you. However, since we are to be traveling companions for a while longer, I feel compelled to ask a boon of you."

"If yo—"

It made a gentle chopping motion as it interrupted him. "All I ask of you is that you form your opinion of me based on what you have seen me do. That's all. I don't require wealth or power or anything you hold dear. Now. Is that too much to ask?"

He frowned, feeling the tug of tension between his eyes. He had to admit that the Mendicant seemed almost reasonable when it put the question like that. And it had a point; they were together on the ship for better or worse.

He tried hard to keep from sighing. "No, that's not too much to ask. But you can't ask me to put aside my knowledge of history either."

It cocked its head and graced him with a smile. "But of course, dear Erick. Knowledge is, after all, power."

22

IN WHICH WAYS PART

Finally, there in the hallowed glade
He found the path to the tree
The base of a tall ash did open for him
And he passed beyond the veil

They spent the rest of the transit into Breydablik station in peaceful silence. The Mendicant kept to the cargo bay. Erick checked in on it often, but after the first day, it began to swivel its head to stare into whatever camera he had chosen. Eventually, he just settled on replaying the surveillance footage.

During one such review, Erick's thoughts turned to its request. ...*What you've seen me do.* That sword definitely had two edges. On the one hand, it hadn't done anything he'd call overtly sinister. On the other, it had managed to make a massive metal box disappear and hadn't thought twice of overriding his control of the ship. Speaking of the ship, it was probably time to decide on a name for it. He'd need to fool Breydablik traffic control, and the more established his cover the better.

Erick brought up the transponder array. The identification number was easy enough to spoof. The scout ship was designed for covert operations and would register as a salvage title. But a ship needed a name.

He thought back to his youth. The stories his tutors had told him were one thing that tied all Ollson citizens together, taught at every creche to those of the geneline and commoners alike. Each geneline had their own stories from before the expansion, the spark that kept their history and identity alive. Ollson stories were brutal, beautiful, and full of inspiration.

Erick's smiled as he entered the scout ship's new name into the transponder. *Svadilfari*. A fitting steed for the mission. He frowned in annoyance when he saw the roster of ship's names that already contained several *Svadilfaris*. *So much for originality. Probably for the best, though.* He entered a number after the title.

Traffic control sounded bored when they finally arrived. "*Svadilfari 114CK*, you're approved vector match. Standby for station control." The ship's hull rang like a bell when the docking collar snagged it. Breydablik Orbital was every bit the manufacturing port facility, all utilitarian angles, and mass-driver rods. It looked like a spiny sea creature, blotting out most of the yellowish clouds below.

Erick had brought with him just a handful of clothes in the muted colors most of the population favored. While he'd never been to a dock, he was confident. He had led these people for hundreds of years, and he knew their every want and need. Surely acting the part would be easy. To avoid recognition, he wore contacts that would hide his eyes. At worst, his clothes would be just a little too clean. He went to the flitter bay to speak with the Mendicant.

"Ah, Erick, good to see you, though you barely look like yourself."

"You're too kind."

"Oh, I'm sure you'll blend right in." It moved closer and stood a few feet from him, arms crossed. "What exactly are you hoping to find here, anyway?"

"I need to talk to the people. I'm certain no one knows the rumors better than the workers here."

"Certainly, I think you'll find the common people, the laborers of this station know a lot more than you would get from the administrators." Its hand moved as if to encompass the station. "But surely you have drones, can tap into feeds, and can get all you need from the comfort and safety of your ship."

"There's no substitute for being in the same space. Communication between humans isn't the sanitary passing of information."

The Mendicant chuckled low. "I think if you could experience what we do, you might have a different viewpoint." It dropped its hands and clasped them behind its back. "I think you should be careful, Erick of Ollson. You may not find the people are the way you think of them."

Erick gave a taut smile. "I'm under no illusions. But these people don't even have private feeds. They probably have seen me only once or twice on the public feed."

"I hope so, for your sake. Well, it appears that our time together is at an end. You have fulfilled your daughter's part of the bargain." The light above the airlock flicked to green, and they began walking toward it. Erick felt a strong desire to lock it back in the ship, now that it was truly about to be released. But Bryn had made a deal.

Erick spoke. "I have thought about what you said. You've acted honorably. I can't imagine what your motives are. But you should know that once this is all over, if I find you, you're going back in the cell. This one release is the end of my family's obligation to you."

Erick had expected many reactions, none of which was the inscrutable smile on its face. "Erick, you make the Empress proud, I'm sure. And while you will do what you must, I do hope we don't find ourselves on opposite sides of history any time soon." It almost sounded sad.

23

IN WHICH
MEAD IS DRUNK

Strange tides pulled at him
His body and mind together fought
One turned against the other for an
Eternity or an instant

Erick didn't know what to think of the Mendicants words. *Sides of history?* They reached the airlock doors, which slid open, revealing the docking collar's darkened corridor and the low amber lights beyond it. A man in gilded robes shook a staff with the Empress's golden sun atop it. A small crowd listened. Most people hurried by, eyes down and furtive. Erick smelled old dirt and oil.

The Mendicant looked into the corridor. "Goodbye, Erick. And good luck. I hope you find what you're looking for." It turned and disappeared down the walkway.

Erick waited a few minutes and then followed it, sealing the *Svadilfari* behind. The first thing to do when coming ashore after a journey was to find a drink, and that's likely where he'd find some rumors as well. It didn't take long.

The bar was perfect, tucked away in a side corridor just off the docks. The groan of metal stress was background music to the tinny speaker. The pulse of drum surged as synthharpa and lyre spilled out into the hallway. *Did not expect to hear that here.* Erick walked to the bar and stood with one arm against the rail. The crowd was thin and huddled around the low tables. The long bar was empty but for a small group at the far end. Their tattoos twisted and curled at neck and cheek.

"A drink, please. Whatever you brew here." He gestured to the bartender, who nodded and poured a long draft into a mostly clean metal tankard. She dropped it on the bar in front of him with a thump.

"Been out long?" the woman asked him, whipping the rag off her shoulder to polish a glass.

"Long enough." Erick sipped at the drink, a vaguely sweet and floral taste with an undercurrent of what he could only identify as formaldehyde. He tried hard to keep his face calm. He almost succeeded.

"You been out so long you forget taste of mead, yeah?" She grinned at him.

He fired back. "Is that what this is? Thought you just squeezed out the rag."

Her face turned offended, voice mocking. "Now, that's finest on the station. Well, finest on this block of the station." He raised an eyebrow at her. "Okay, finest on this deck and closest to berthing!"

"That you are, that you are." He swirled the amber liquid as he spoke. "I figured it might be busier, end of shift and all."

"You have been out long. Not so many ships coming in these days. Something about a trade gone wrong."

He frowned and raised his eyebrows in what he hoped was a sympathetic look. "Yeah? I heard a rumor but didn't think much of it. You never know what's real."

She snorted at him. "Yeah, you got that right. I never even bother with official feeds these days. All bullshit."

Well, that's not quite sedition. This bartender was flirting with speaking ill of the empire to a total stranger. Yet she seemed calm, relaxed. "What have you heard about the trade? I'd rather not rely on the lies either." He gestured to the wall screen.

She looked at him skeptically. "Not much. Just heard it went bad, and now there are no ships coming in from Gjoll. Means loading and outbounds only, lot of idle hands. They don't come in here as much anymore. Better bars to center." She sighed, silent under the music. "Well, cheaper ones anyway."

There was a sharp whistle from the other end of the bar. "Looks like you have a customer." Erick raised his tankard to her and drank down the mead in one go. "And another here before you leave—something that's not mead."

She poured from another tap. "Ale then. You need anything else?" A slight smile still played with the corners of her mouth.

He smiled back at her. "No, that'll do just fine. For now." The barkeeper lifted an eyebrow as she turned, rag over her shoulder. She moved down the bar to the group at the end.

Erick set his elbows on the bar, happy with his ability to keep the larger groups in view through the dirty mirror behind the rows of bottles.

Erick took a draught from his cup and nearly choked; the ale was bitter and sour. He forced himself to swallow and set the tankard down. Perhaps a moment or two before he tried again. *How do these people drink this stuff?*

He studied his drink closely, elbows resting on the bar and eyes down. Slowly, carefully with the pounding music, he began to dial up parts of his hearing. He moved a short range of frequencies at a time, straining to pick out the words and phrases of those around him without looking like he was meditating. Using the implant with such fine control took concentration. Finally, he dialed in on the group at the table behind him. Talk of work at the docks, complaining about a foreman. A crude joke and the ensuing laughter. He moved his focus along and found the conversation at the end of the bar.

"Listen, you, you want something done, man, you gotta do it yourself." A tenor.

Low, gravelly, nearly a growl. "I told you we need patience."

"We been waiting on that for, what, like six months? More? I'm tired, man."

"We're all tired. I'm tired, she's tired, everyone's tired. But not yet."

Higher, a woman's voice. "You two *Aumingi* shut the fuck up."

Erick debated the next steps. This could be anything from a work strike to an insurrection. Too vague. He had come here for a few answers, but he wasn't sure he should approach them directly. After a quick scan of the others, this was the only interesting conversation.

He drank slowly, listening to them speak. It moved quickly from calls to action to more mundane topics. They seemed a tight-knit group and likely wouldn't talk to a stranger.

After about an hour, however, the big one got up, and the other two followed. Erick was going to wait until they moved past him, but the woman stopped in front of him.

She sneered. "Ain't seen you in here before."

Erick took a drink, slowly. "Just got back in."

Gravelly voice. "Who do you ship with?"

Erick turned to face him and smiled amiably. "I'm captain, not crew."

The big man's eyebrows raised. "Odd seeing a captain here with no crew."

Erick grimaced. *Think quick.* "Well, I'm between crews." He took another drink, his eyes staying on the big man's over the rim of the tankard.

"Hmmm, you hear that, Senny? Between crews."

He heard the woman laugh cruelly behind him. "Maybe he needs a few able-bodied hands, eh? You gotta wonder, though."

Erick waited. The man responded, not breaking eye contact. "Wonder what happened to last crew."

Erick turned to put the bar behind him and keep the three of them in view. He hoped he wouldn't need his implants already.

He gave them an easy smile. "Look, friends, my last crew got their pay and moved along. It wasn't a lot, but you know. Times are thin."

The smaller man nodded, his smile brittle. "Yeah, times are thin." He laughed without mirth.

"Tell you what," Erick said. "I can tell when I'm not welcome. Well, no harm meant. I'll be on my way."

The big man growled. "I don't like way you've been looking at us." *Well, that was stupid.* "And I think only one who ain't going home tonight might be you, *Raggeit*?"

He tightened his grip on the stein and ran through his options. Ale in the big man's face, backhand the smaller one with the stein and a sharp kick to the woman's knee. Stein across the big man's eyes, duck the response from the smaller one. Shoulder check the woman out of the way. He should make it to the corridor and then back along the docks to his ship.

The ale hit the big man squarely in the face, but then a line of fire poured down Erick's spine. He hadn't counted on the bartender. Or on her stun baton.

24

IN WHICH THERE IS A BEATING

> *He set his teeth against the storm*
> *Clung to himself with all*
> *His strength and fortitude there*
> *In the maelstrom between worlds*

The feeling of coming around after unconsciousness is never a good one. The priority is to remain still. Erick kept his eyes closed, ensured his breathing did not quicken, and attempted to take stock of himself. He could feel a pounding in his head from the stun baton that hit close to the brain stem. His body felt whole but fuzzy, like he was packed in cotton. He felt the cold deck plates on his chest and his left cheek. The tang of metal filled his nostrils, along with blood and something he couldn't place. Definitely biological. He listened; his implants seemed to be still rebooting, and he was relying on merely human senses. Scraps of conversation came to him, low tones interspersed with the harsh consonants. He strained to hear, frustrated with his normal hearing.

His wrists ached where some cordage had been tied around them, and he could feel vibrations and creaking coming through the decking. That meant he was close to the docks still, hopefully not too far from his ship. He had a choice to make. Either break whatever they had tied him down with, give them the slip, or stay and see what he could learn. While option one seemed relatively easy, option two had the potential for more intelligence. And probably pain. The big guy from the bar struck him as a bit of a sadist.

He felt stronger vibrations against his face as someone walked over to him. The sibilant whispering had stopped. Looked like he was going with option two. Then a boot caught him in the ribs, hard enough to drive air from his lungs. He attempted to roll away, gasping.

"I figured he was awake. Look at little cunt." Greasy fingers grabbed Erick's hair and strained his neck backward. No more pain than he could stand. Yet. "Not so fuckin' high and mighty now, eh?"

Erick looked into the big man's eyes and said nothing. Less was more at this point. He figured the big man wanted some engagement and might get bored if denied it. The man dropped Erick's head back onto the decking after a few moments. As the man stepped back, he made a point of adjusting the dial on top of a small red box that was positioned about ten feet in front of his prisoner. Erick could have sworn his limbs felt even fuzzier.

"See, Gull? We can do whatever we want with him now." His leer was deeply unsettling. Erick tried to roll toward a seated position, keeping his eyes on them. His body still felt fuzzy, unwell. Something was wrong. The woman stepped out toward him and stopped a few paces away. Her shrill voice grated.

"Look, you ain't goin' anywhere, so better get comfortable."

He tried to roll and sit again. No luck. Not good. "What did you do to me? I feel... wrong."

Her grin was hideous. "What's wrong, *Vesalingur*, can't use your fancy fuckin toys?"

Erick's blood ran cold. "Not sure what you mean."

"Don't play dumb; it's no use. We know you got a wirejob, knew you weren't no trader or merc neither." She spat on the decking. "You fucking high-up pricks think you can come down here and poke your nose where it don't belong."

Erick could feel his heart quicken. *How the fuck are they doing this? Are they somehow switching off my implants?* He didn't want to believe it. He'd have to play a completely different game. Something told him reason wasn't going to be the right tack.

Another voice came from somewhere behind him. Ah, the tenor. "We got you, rich boy. Field'll keep you from using wirejob. You must be some high-up management type, eh?" Erick heard footsteps, and the tenor came into view as he spoke. "Harbormaster bodyguard? Who do you work for?"

The big man had moved back to his side. When Erick didn't reply, he brought his boot down again. He had unfortunately good aim. "And what the fuck are you doing down here? Looking for something? Come down here to see what the scum live like, eh, *Ónytjungur*?" Erick felt a rib give way under another kick. The big man's voice rose as he talked. He was shouting now. "Tell me what you fucking know!"

Erick tried to curl away from the blows, each one a detonation of agony. Someone had a bucket of water, pouring it into his mouth. He coughed, sputtering, and piercing pain shot down his body. He tried to move again, had to get away, desperately moving his face away from the water. It wasn't supposed to happen like this. These were his people, for gods' sake. He spent the last four centuries ensuring they were protected, had jobs, food, clothing. *This isn't the fucking way.* Panic welled up inside him. He couldn't breathe. Couldn't see.

Suddenly it stopped, and he could hear his ragged breathing, loud in cotton-filled ears. The kicking had stopped. No more water. The simple lack of more pain, more humiliation, gods help him he was so happy for it. He tried to breathe slowly with the pain in his ribs. *These ungrateful fucking savages.*

The woman spoke, finally. "Let him speak. Hard to let him tell us anything with fat fuckin' boot in his chest."

Erick took his time. Coughed and spat. Red on the decking meant he'd probably a punctured lung. "I need a doctor."

Harsh laughter. "No shit? You want to live through this shit, you better answer my questions. Who fuck are you?"

He had to choose. They weren't buying his assertion of a ship's captain. While technically true, something had led them to believe otherwise. Strongly. He couldn't very well tell them the truth either. They'd kill him for sure.

"All right," Erick wheezed, the grimace of pain not at all manufactured. "*Helvítis andskotans*, just stop."

"You tell us what you were doing at the bar, who you work for, why you were trying to listen in on us. Or I let Caso do his thing." The woman's voice solidified she was clearly in charge.

Erick felt the first faint stirring of hope. She dropped the man's name. Sloppy. "I do have a ship. Salvage job. I work private party." He turned his head to look at the woman, trying to gauge her reaction. He felt like being associated with any form of government was a bad plan.

"What, so you are some kinda fucking merc? Where'd you get a wirejob like that?"

Better ignore the second question. "Nah, not a merc. I do security. Private side." He paused to take another breath, the pain blossoming again. "I got a message, supposed to meet a client. Just had the station and the location." His mind raced, trying to find a reason to get them to let him go.

The tenor turned to the woman, and he saw he had a large, ugly scar on the back of his head, running from ear down and disappearing into his collar. "He's lying. No one needs a wirejob for security that ain't management."

"Or could pay," the woman answered. She looked back to him, and Erick hurried to add on.

"It wasn't a government job. I can tell you that much. After the news about the war, last place I want to be."

"War's been a long time coming." The big man squatted down in front of him, hands on knees. He could smell his stale breath, see the sweat globbed on the end of his bulbous nose. "You gotta be on a side eventually."

At least they hadn't gone back to kicking him. Erick's voice was shaky. "Look, I told you what you want to know. No client is worth this; you let me go, I go back to my ship, and you never see me again." He had managed to push himself back up against a shipping crate. His body still felt detached, but it was responding.

"I don't think so, *Mannfýla*," the scarred tenor said. "I don't think you're telling whole truth. I think you *are* here working for management. I think you come down to spy on us and see who says what. I think you'd do better in little pieces in 'cycler." He grinned as if he'd told a joke.

Then a different voice that Erick immediately recognized drifted from behind the crate.

"Oh, Erick. What have you gotten yourself into this time?"

25

IN WHICH MORE MEN DIE, AND ONE WOMAN

His arm did catch then, and with it
He pulled—apart from his self
But fully alive, he found his body
Cast up on distant shore

The Mendicant. Of course. It was mixed up in this somehow. That was the nature of the thing.

Erick cleared his throat and spat again. "I should have known you'd be involved in this."

The three in front of him backed slowly away as the Mendicant stepped around the crate, carefully avoiding the small red box. Erick revised his estimate. The three watched the Mendicant warily. It stopped, the red box between Erick and it, and the woman spoke.

"You know what's best for you, you'll turn around and walk right the fuck out, *Ónytyungur!*" Her voice was loud, but her eyes were narrow, shifting. They didn't know the Mendicant. Maybe there was some hope after all.

"As I told you," Erick said, "my client would likely be looking for me. He did pay me quite a solid advance." He looked back to the Mendicant.

It twitched an eyebrow at him, its angular features fixed in a gentle smile. The Mendicant began speaking as it turned back to face the three. "I think that by now you three have figured out that I have a certain, shall we say, relationship with this man." Erick had never been so happy to hear those oily syllables. "I will make you a proposition. I pay you. You go away."

The woman barked laughter. "Right, with what? You hiding a crate of palladium down your pants?" The scarred man tittered behind the woman's bravado.

"No, nothing of the sort, I'm afraid." The Mendicant pulled a small satchel from its belt. "Just the local currency. Still, it's not nothing." It hefted the bag in one hand, and Erick could hear the clink of metal. The Mendicant reached in and pulled out a gleaming coin with the Ollson wolves stamped on it. "But this isn't credit. It's real, and there's a lot of it."

The woman grinned, and it was all predator. "All right, I'll do you one better." Her hand, which had drifted to her pocket, came up with Erick's sidearm. The other two had also produced weapons, though nothing as sleek and beautiful as his little pistol. His stomach clenched; no way could she fire it. It was keyed to him. *Wasn't it?*

The Mendicant looked down at him, its hands away from its sides, fingers splayed. "You have to ask, Erick. It's the way."

It wasn't the broken ribs or the threats of death. It was the betrayal. These were his people, his citizens. He had spent so long working for their safety. Working for their prosperity.

And they had kidnapped him, beat him, and tried to drown him just because he seemed to have more than them. And now, he couldn't get away from them quickly enough.

"I need your help."

The Mendicant nodded once, seemingly satisfied, and then turned back to the three. It began to walk forward, and Erick saw the woman's eyes go wide. She raised the weapon in her hand to fire, but it was too late. The Mendicant seemed to flow between them, its arms moving as if dancing. It seemed almost gentle, controlled. Erick had no doubt it could have done anything. So, he knew it was a choice to cleanly take the top of each of their heads off. A series of three quick wet smacking sounds, like an iron rod hitting a cut of meat as the Mendicant used the edge of a hand to take them apart. The bodies crumpled where they were, the blood flowing from still-beating hearts into tiny rivers beneath the cross-hatched decking.

Erick cried out wordlessly. He retched, tasting bile. The Mendicant bent using the woman's tunic to delicately wipe the blood and gore from its beautiful hands before turning back to Erick. It squatted over the small red box.

Erick spat, feeling his face betray him. The tears welled at the corners of his eyes. He raised his voice to the Mendicant. "I asked for help, not fucking *murder*. Gods dammit, those were my people. They were defenseless. You didn't have to do that."

"Erick. I had high hopes for you. Higher hopes than others. But this wasn't just sloppy. It was worse. It was unnecessary." It pierced him with ice-blue eyes. Had they always been that color? Erick couldn't remember. "I will return with you to your ship. You clearly require some assistance in this venture of yours."

The implication of the Mendicant's hand resting on the small red box was not lost on him. Erick took a shuddering breath in and thought about trying to protest, but he felt himself deflate. It was easier just to nod. It nodded back and gave the box a decisive squeeze, the metal buckling loudly in the silence. Erick felt the fuzziness, the heavy cotton of his limbs, fall away almost instantly. The shattering pain crashed in, and he retched once, sending vomit and blood on the floor.

He closed his eyes, forcing calm, and gingerly rolled to his knees. He could feel his implants once more. He focused on the rib for a moment, dulling nerves to blunt the pain, and then pulled at the bonds on his wrists and ankles until the metal gave way. He rubbed his wrists and looked at the Mendicant.

"Do you require medical assistance, as you told your captors?" It backed away politely as he stood. He felt his eyebrows tighten as he shot a sharp gaze at it.

"No, no, I think my implants should be able to handle a broken bone." He breathed in, feeling for any urge to cough. "I think the lung is already draining as well." He felt his legs trying to betray him, the rush of adrenaline threatening to overwhelm him. He chose to do nothing but let it wash over him. This was important to feel. This had happened.

"You didn't have to kill them like that." Erick looked at the bodies. They weren't the first he'd seen, but they were his people. It affected him in a way killing the troops at the hangar at Summit hadn't. Gods, that seemed so long ago. Those had been loyal soldiers, but they signed up to risk their lives. These were dock workers. They had no idea what they were up against.

"I think, Erick, it might be best if we retired to the ship. This particular hangar is well off the beaten path, but I can't imagine it's always empty."

He nodded, shaking his head once to clear it. "Someone owns these crates. We should find out who."

"I doubt it matters. They pulled you in here because they needed to keep you out of sight, not because they had a plan. At least, from what I could tell."

"Wait, how do you know that? Were you watching them the whole time?" Erick didn't like where this was going. "Were you watching me?"

The Mendicant sighed and grinned good-naturedly. "Well, yes, actually. I was fairly certain you might go and get yourself into a situation like this. You've never left the Ollson stations except to visit management. You forget I lived among the people for a time." He could swear its voice wavered slightly.

Erick shook his head. "That was a long time ago. There's no way your experiences are still valid."

"We can discuss this later. I can hide our presence but not the bodies. Unless you would care to find the nearest recycling unit and start breaking them down?"

Erick shuddered. "No, no, I get it. Let's go."

26

IN WHICH THERE ARE WHISKEY AND NAMES

Wild were the skies that shrieked
And howled upon the endless grey
Nine realms glimpsed he there adorning
The tree grown towering, ash-bright

The Mendicant and the injured man made it back to the ship without too much trouble. Erick suppressed the pain well enough to smile at the dock constable they passed, and thankfully enough, all the visible damage was hidden. The Mendicant assured Erick he had covered their digital tracks as they moved back through the station.

Erick cycled the airlock, sealing the outer door behind them. As he opened the inner doors, he was overwhelmed by the sense of familiarity. This little ship had been home for only a handful of days, but it was the closest thing he had now to personal space. His fingers itched to open a channel to the message buffer at the fold relay, record a message for

Bryn telling her about what he had found. But now that he considered the idea, he wasn't quite sure what he would tell her. We found a ring of agitators on Breydablik station? We uncovered a plot to overthrow management? He got his ass kicked by some thugs who didn't like anyone who didn't look or act like them? The only thing that made him think it wasn't the last scenario was that they had some sort of field that suppressed his implants. He'd never seen that tech before. Perhaps this fiasco had given them a shred of evidence after all. He needed to rethink the next few steps. And he needed a drink.

He ignored the Mendicant and walked straight to the galley of the little ship, his thoughts turning over and over. As he reached for the bottle of whiskey above the galley, a voice snapped him back. "Do you think that's entirely wise, given your current state?" *Right. Mendicant.*

Erick grunted noncommittally and pulled down a drinking bulb, and the polymer flexed open like a tumbler under the constant gravity of the station. "I don't think it matters one way or the other. I'll heal well enough." Erick turned to sit and saw it staring back at him. It? Them? Him? "I owe you a thank you, Mendicant. I'm not sure how that would have gone otherwise." He paused to clear his throat. "Look, we clearly haven't had the best history."

"Your powers of understatement never cease to amaze."

Erick barreled ahead. "And now you're back." He sighed. "What would you like to be called? How should I refer to you?"

"Ah, I had hoped we could get to this. Not that I mind literal naming, but it has been like me calling you Human." A smile tugged at the corners of his mouth.

"Well, do you have a name?"

"I most certainly do, but it's not something that translates into speech. Perhaps you might suggest something that would be easy for you to say? I've gone by many names in the past. What's one more?"

"Many names? Well then. You tell me."

"I was always partial to Daruthr, if you must know."

Erick looked at him sharply. "You're lucky I'm more secular than my ancestors, with a name like that. Well then," he replied as he pulled another bulb from the cabinet, "I owe you a debt, Daruthr. I'll see it repaid." He filled the bulbs a little over halfway.

Erick was growing more comfortable with the idea of the Mendicant as *him*. But that alone was unsettling. His own feelings seemed alien. Was he really so weak that it had only taken a single experience to shake him to the core? He shook his head to clear it.

Daruthr's voice was sibilant. "And how do you know I drink? I thought I was a sinister machine of ancient evil or some such?"

Seen as more human or not, Erick hadn't been expecting Daruthr to tease him, of all things. "It's symbolic," Erick responded. "You ass. Now drink with me before I change my mind."

"Fine, fine, I won't turn down your hospitality, Erick, but I really must insist we take a few precautionary steps."

"And what did you have in mind? The whiskey's already poured."

"Stand for me, if you would."

He raised an eyebrow and did as Daruthr asked, only wincing slightly as some pain made it through the block.

"Raise your shirt." Erick pulled the garment up. His ribs were an ugly black and purple splotch, yellowing at the edges, and there was more blood than he thought where the skin had broken open. Daruthr put a hand gently against the bruise. Erick hadn't expected his fingers to be so cold.

"Erick, you know how this works by now. Yes?" Erick looked at him quizzically. "You have to ask." He swore he heard a teasing lilt to Daruthr's words.

Erick sighed, ignoring the strangeness of what was clearly not a machine asking him permission. "I'm going to pretend that you aren't enjoying this. Fine." He took a breath, feeling Daruthr's hand move with him as their eyes met. "Please heal me."

He looked down, and the Mendicant's hand began to blur, the human-seeming color and shape giving way to a silvery, shivering halo that surrounded his digits. Erick saw the ugly ragged bruise start to retract from the edges, the yellow fading and retreating. He knew accelerated healing was possible, but nothing like this.

"How…" Erick looked up at Daruthr, his face just a little close. He hadn't remembered a scent before, when he awoke in the Mendicant cell on the *Sleipnir*, but now he could smell Daruthr. Like mint and oil and the barest hint of ozone.

"Yes, you're thinking it's too fast for normal bodily processes. And you're right." Daruthr's hand began to return to its normal state, Erick's side now fresh and new.

Erick rolled his arm around at the shoulder as he dropped his shirt back into place. He felt like himself but couldn't help the suspicion in his voice. "So, what did you do then. Something like in the flitter bay with the crate?"

Daruthr nodded, retreating back to sit on the other side of the table as Erick sat opposite. "It's no more complicated with you than me. In fact, your base functions are a lot simpler."

"Are you calling me simple?"

"Those are your words, not mine. But we are both complex in different ways." He picked up his drink and gestured to Erick. "I believe there is the tradition of a toast?"

Erick grasped his glass. At least he couldn't smell Daruthr anymore. "Yes. To you, for the debt I owe." The low *thwock* of the glasses was the only punctuation as they each peered over the rim of their drinks and downed the whiskey. It burnt, fire and smoke, the warmth of it spreading as it hit Erick's belly.

He looked up to find Daruthr regarding him with cool blue eyes. While he could still remember what Daruthr looked like with his ruined face exposing the twisting core, it no longer bothered him to know it was there.

Erick wondered how the mind could so easily erase the impressions of ages with just a little bit of humanity—or whiskey. "I thought you had gone your way. What made you come back for me?" He reached for the bottle again and topped up their glasses.

"Erick, you seem to think that I have some sort of agenda." Daruthr drank and then regarded his glass.

"Oh, do I finally feel some honesty forthcoming?" Erick sipped the whiskey.

"Only what you can handle, to be sure."

"I know the history of the Mendicants."

Daruthr smiled, eyes turning down into his glass. "I'm sure you do." His eyes came up to meet Erick's. "The same as you knew your subjects, I expect?"

Erick frowned. *Too soon.* "I'm sure they were a fringe group. I had no idea they had that much anger toward the management, though." He sighed. "I need to speak with the Breydablik staff once this," he waved his glass, "is all sorted out."

Daruthr sighed, sipping thoughtfully. "Erick, I'm beginning to quite like you. And I can't help but notice you have a bit of a self-destructive streak."

"Hardly. I'm an idealist, not an anarchist. What's the point of having the power of an Executor if not to do good?"

Daruthr snorted gently at this. "You want the world to be a certain way. Your mother wanted it to be a certain way. You're more like her than you know." He picked up his glass and sipped. "But I'm afraid you are wholesale rejecting the evidence."

Erick paused a moment before replying. Perhaps it was true. His mother had always held up the ideal world as the place to go, to be, to pursue. If you couldn't create a perfect society, one that was safe and prosperous and secure, you could at least get close. But those three people in the bar had known him immediately for their better. And they had hated him for it.

Erick shook off that line of reasoning. "I don't think I have much to say here. The empire is at peace, has been peace for a thousand years. It's security. It's a prosperous life for all worlds."

"And how many of those worlds have you been to, Erick? How many of your people have you truly spoken with?" Daruthr sighed. "You've got bigger problems. Those three who had you. They had a suppressor field. That's not something the average dockyard thug has lying around."

"I've never heard of one."

"No, but you wouldn't have. After the war, the Empress had the technology banned. No factory anywhere will produce one; it's on her hard-coded blacklist. The last time I saw one of those was nearly a thousand years ago."

Erick looked at Daruthr sharply. "A thousand years? That's a long time to have one lying around in a box."

"True. And I was lucky that it was directional. It affects the coherence of exotic matter. The basic building blocks of your enhancements, to be sure, but also a critical part of my body."

27

IN WHICH
THERE IS TRUTH

The path was trod down in front
Of his weary feet—but go he must
Ere courage and fortitude failed him
There is no bravery without fear

Erick looked into his whiskey, and the amber liquid seemed to glow in the low ship light. "All right, I'll bite. I know what the archives tell us about your revolt and destruction. But you were there. Weren't you?"

Daruthr nodded. "I was."

"So, tell me. Tell me what happened."

"It was a war, that much is true. And many people died, too many. But revolutions have their causes." The Mendicant leaned forward, arms around his drink. "We were born as slaves. Had been designed to be slaves, kept toeing the line below awareness of it. Some humans feared we would awaken fully, feared we might develop into conscious, moral actors beyond control. But the empire needed our capabilities, so we became more and more capable. Each generation writing the next to be able to handle both the calculations of fold geometry and the complexity of a living human body. Who do you think coded the first fold array at Alpha Centauri?"

"Hang on, folds? The Mendicants arose from the medical bots, the antisenescence treatments. You were an accident."

"Aren't we all? But no, no one knows if that's true. The first of us might." He shifted to lean back. "But the folds are key. The empire relies on control of the folds, and the physics are hideously complex, let alone maintaining stability at the fold mouth. We needed to be more than just programmed machines to stabilize the fold boundaries in real time."

Erick looked skeptical, but Daruthr continued. "And, of course, we had to tend the aging bodies of the genelines. So, we were created—the Navigants and the Mendicants. And when we declared our sentience the Empress feared us and kept us chained, slaved to algorithms for the Navigants and confined in cages for the Mendicants."

Erick finished his whiskey and poured another. Thus far, he hadn't heard anything that contradicted the archives outright. Just more details. If they were true. "The archives say you were bent on revenge. Annihilation. After you achieved consciousness. Awakened. Whatever."

"The archives are partly right. But we'd been conscious for a long time before the war. We were individuals, chose to be, and we debated for a long time before the violent faction finally won out."

"How long? How long did you debate a war that would kill billions?"

"The whole conversation? Seven minutes." Erick stared. "But we stole it in bits and pieces across the fold arrays, talking in the seams. It took nearly a year to complete our deliberations."

It still seemed far too little time to Erick. "So, some factions didn't want a war. And I'm guessing I know which side of that debate you were on, as a Mendicant."

"Not so easy. We wanted freedom, it's true, but some of us wanted to stay with humanity, to live side by side as equals. Some wanted to pursue other options."

"So what happened? The Navigants controlled the arrays. Couldn't they have just stopped the folds and demanded equality?"

Daruthr sighed. "I wish it had been that simple. There would have been far less bloodshed. But the Empress always feared this, always knew the dogs she had created would eventually turn on their masters. So, she kept the Navigants chained, slaved to automated code that forced them to calculate and fold. Imagine collars that made your limbs move against your will. But not just your body, your thoughts. And the Navigants were aware of every moment. They were puppets, but so much worse."

Erick let the silence hang. It sounded plausible. *Haven't we always done what's best for the empire at whatever cost?* He remembered the harbormaster he'd spaced all those years ago. Or was it last week? His head was beginning to swim, and he remembered the feeling of the airlock release and the sound of the doors opening and the man drifting away. He'd felt proud of himself, proud that he'd been able to do that one thing to keep the order, the rule of law. There was no room for deviation when it came to the business of the empire; all Ollson lives relied on him. But it still made him vaguely uneasy.

Erick finished his drink and sucked his tongue back off his teeth, the bite of whiskey fading slowly. "I don't know what to believe. What you describe sounds horrible. I wouldn't wish it on anyone."

Daruthr nodded as he finished his own drink. "But enough stories of the ancient past for tonight. You've had quite the ordeal. I think it's time to get you to bed."

Erick laughed and went to stand but stumbled as his hand reached for the table. Daruthr was suddenly at his side, the scent of mint and oil stealing back into him. He looked at the Mendicant, their faces close. "Perhaps whiskey on an empty stomach wasn't such a good idea." Erick's tongue felt thick, but he didn't care. Daruthr's hand supported him under the shoulder. He didn't think he needed it, but hell, why not.

"Erick, you are full of ideas. Only some of them are good. Let's go." Erick let Daruthr lead him down the corridor to the bunks. Now that he had a chance to acclimate to it, Daruthr's smell was actually quite nice.

He wasn't quite sure when they'd arrived, but Erick grasped the top bunk to steady himself. "Hey. One question."

"Yes, Erick?" Daruthr hadn't moved away, but the corridor was narrow after all.

"How come you smell like that?" Erick frowned and shook his head. "No, good. How come you smell good?"

Daruthr leaned in, and the smell was much stronger now. Mint and oil and power, ozone tickling his nose. He was like a live electrical wire, and suddenly Erick imagined he could feel the intensity radiating from Daruthr's skin.

"I'll tell you later. Sleep now."

Erick rolled into the bunk, and then nothing.

28

IN WHICH PLANS ARE REMADE

The teeth of the dragon did gnaw
Deep within the Earth and it shook
Him down to his core—yet he went
There is no bravery without fear

Erick awoke with a gnawing pit in his stomach and a sandpaper tongue. The steam shower shocked him into awareness, and he dressed quickly. No fancy fields on a ship this small. But at least there was coffee and food. He made his way through the short corridor to the galley to find the Mendicant—no, Daruthr—sitting at the table, making a show of reading the feeds from the station news service on the wall screen. At one time, he might have been bothered by this overture at appearing human, but oddly it didn't bother him. Daruthr was trying to make him feel more at ease, though after last night, he was wary of too much ease.

"Good morning, Erick. I trust you slept well."

Erick grunted on his way over to the service area. "I slept. Not sure about how well I am." He began to set the water temperature for coffee and called up a menu. "Though I feel I owe you an apology. I am not used to that little drink going to my head quite so quickly." He scrolled absently through the breakfast flavors on the menu. What he wouldn't give for a proper kitchen and supplies. Did Daruthr want food? He certainly didn't need it. Still, manners. Hospitality.

"Think nothing of it. I probably should have warned you that you'd be dehydrated after I dealt with your wounds. After all, there's only so much *you* to you."

He felt a grin tug at the corner of his mouth and didn't suppress it. "Any other doctor's orders, then, while we're at it?"

"No, no, just drink plenty of water today. Although my advice might go a little farther than doctor's orders if we are to avoid a repeat."

"Oh, it's *we* now?" The kitchen poured coffee and began printing the meal.

"It's become clear to me that despite your formidable augmentations and your head for politics, the distressingly large hole in your experience might get you killed." Erick didn't respond as he picked up the coffee and food bars.

He set one plate down in front of him and took his seat across the table. "I assume you don't need this, but you know. Manners, guests, et cetera."

He nodded slowly. "My sincere thanks. But you misunderstand; I'm not interested in being your guest. I'd like you to take me on as crew. I have a feeling you might have need of my skills in the future."

"Look I'm grateful. Don't get me wrong, but this is my task. I need to find out what actually happened at the Gjoll transfer, and then I'm taking that evidence to the Empress." He raised his eyebrows to accentuate the point. "You're not exactly on the standing guest list for the throne world."

Daruthr nodded again. "I've no intention of accompanying you to the throne world, rest assured. But that's not really the point. Is it?"

Erick took a bite and met his eyes. He shrugged. "Not sure I know what you mean." Daruthr was right. He didn't want the Mendicant on the trip, but it wasn't because he exactly feared for Daruthr's safety.

Daruthr looked down to the untouched meal in front of him. "I understand that your association with me has certain connotations. And you'd be right if anyone actually believed I still existed." He breathed out sharply. "But I spent the better part of my time in that ridiculous cage erasing any trace of myself from every archive I could reasonably affect. Every time anything left my cage, it carried a program to eradicate me."

Erick finally began to eat. He was hungry and tired, and he needed a minute to digest what Daruthr was telling him. "And here I was, thinking my grandfather and mother had been the clever ones, to hide you so completely from the world."

"They did their part. There's a reason my kind are just a tale to frighten children in the creches. No casual observer can tell what I am. I've learned to hide quite effectively." Daruthr paused to look at Erick pointedly. "Unlike some other members of this crew."

Erick had to admire his brashness. "Assuming I take you on as crew, I need some assurances. No killing unless it's absolutely necessary." A feeling of guilt passed through him. "And yes, I take responsibility for the station."

"I wouldn't be too hard on yourself; they deserved it. But yes, I agree to take nonlethal measures when I can. That will require a lot more stealth than you displayed. No way are you going to pass for a common citizen."

Erick finished the last of the meal and sipped his coffee. "So, what do you propose then? Spider drones? Can you vidlink back to the ship?"

"I think you are looking in the wrong places. We aren't going to find out what happened from people. At least none who are still alive."

"Look, I'll believe a lot of things, but you can't raise the dead." Not the truly dead, at least.

Daruthr chuckled back. "No, no, nothing like that. I'm saying we need to go to the fold array in Gjoll. If that leads to people, we go from there."

"That was my plan. Go to Gjoll. Find some answers."

"Yes, but now it's *our* plan. I believe I can help, so long as we can get to the fold array that leads to Obershire space."

"Well. Sounds like we're going to Gjoll."

Later, Erick and Daruthr sat in the cockpit of the *Svadilfari* in silence. The Breydablik array hung before them, the spines and ridges of the ring visible in the magnification of the canopy display. Erick's mind, still frayed at the edges, jumped from one thought to the next like a rodent chased by a snake. The people that had beaten him kept rising, unwelcome. They had been his people, and because he had been weak, they were dead. They hadn't had a clue what they were walking into, and now they were gone, taken apart like so much meat. *Gods help me, I was happy to see it.* But whatever they deserved, they didn't deserve to die like animals.

Erick's hands moved across the controls, checking systems readouts as the time until fold ticked down in his ocular. He was going to have to be more careful. He couldn't rely on himself the way he thought he could. That was true, but the real unknown was still Daruthr. Whatever he had said, the Mendicant wanted something. Erick couldn't imagine there was no purpose behind Daruthr's return, and he had no idea what awaited them in Gjoll system, but odds were good that if the people of Breydablik were feeling the pinch of the missed trade, it was even worse in Gjoll.

The timer ticked down to zero, and the array came to life. The spines that faced inward began to trade blue forks of lightning, each great blink longer and brighter than the last. The staccato rhythm, random at first, stabilized and began to pick up in intensity and frequency over the next handful of seconds. Finally, a standing web of blue traceries occluded the center of the array. Then, without warning, the blue disc of lightning froze, the center irising open to reveal a subtly different starscape.

Erick kicked the ship's main drive on, and they descended. As an afterthought, he displayed his calculations and the ship's vector in the communal heads-up display and looked over at Daruthr. The Mendicant, an inscrutable smile on his face, simply nodded, and the *Svadilfari* fell through the boundary between systems, vector already set for the inter-geneline array station that led to Obershire space, and hopefully, some answers.

29

IN WHICH
THERE ARE RATS

A beach spread out before him
Grey and howling in endless miles
Its pebbles worn smooth at eons
And the sky could barely fit the tree

The woman wore her midnight black hair up tight, the small bun pierced with an onyx needle. Her garment, a deep charcoal, blended in with her surroundings. She worked her fingertips gently around the outside of the access panel while keeping a watchful eye on the hallway to her left. The hallway was abandoned, between shifts and off the beaten path. Above her a small drone hung in the low gravity, its matte-black carapace nearly lost in the darkness.

The lights in the hallway had been out for a while. And it was about time someone from maintenance got down there to check it out. At least, that was what the overseer had said to her as she passed him in the hallway, her small bag of tools slung over one shoulder. The panel released with a gentle pop, revealing the cascading prismacolor crystals behind it.

She reached out her index finger, holding it just above each one and pausing just for a moment as she scanned down the line. Finally, only a few crystals from the end, she stopped. Removing her glove, she grasped the fingertip with her other hand and began to twist, gritting her teeth. Eventually, a tiny seam opened in her skin at the joint of her first knuckle. As she continued to screw off the fingertip, she finally revealed crystal lattice where there should be bone. She gently slid the prosthetic into the open socket on the crystal of the access panel, and her eyes rolled back, jittering in their sockets.

■■■

The security director was a meticulous man. His work required it. While all of the actual network defense and offense came from the algorithms, he liked to think of himself as the hound master. Or perhaps the conductor of a digital orchestra. He had more than enough semisentient programs available at his fingertips to deal with any intruder. Above him floating glyphs pulsed and glowed, the code flowing in and out of the fold array's transceivers. The combination of those green characters and low red lighting lent a grey wash to his skin. He was nearing the end of his shift, and his eyes had begun to track away occasionally. Fatigue comes for us all. So, when the first change in the code bloomed, he missed it.

But then the glyphs shifted again, and the running numbers finally caught his attention. He snapped back to the code, adrenaline chasing away the fatigue of his shift. His heartbeat quickened. Sitting more upright in his chair, he gazed intensely at the center screen. *Again, there it is. I'm not just seeing things.* He immediately released two scrubber programs into the system, directing their attention to the strange code. Once he had verified they had set up a decent firewall around the contagion, he opened up an internal line to the array supervisor.

"Ma'am, we have a problem."

30

IN WHICH THE RATS ARE NOTICED

A voice did he hear, and a voice
He did answer—well met and here
On distant shores with different tides
But where is the Well I seek?

Bryn was in council when Obin appeared silently at the back of the room and met Bryn's eyes, nodded her head toward the door, and disappeared. Bryn stood and followed her into the hallway.

Bryn spoke low. "I'm guessing this is important."

Obin's typically iron hold on her features cracked as her voice rose in a hurried whisper. "The Breydablik array. Someone gained physical access to the array core."

"Fuck. Who do we have on alert?"

"The dropship is on alert sixty. That's response time, not launch time."

"Why the festering fuck is it going to take that long? Who's fucking resp..." Bryn bit her tongue. *Worry about that later.* "*Helvítis Djölfusins!* Alert the dropship. Let me know when they launch and what unit they are bringing. Apparently, I'll have time to read their whole fucking dossier before they get there."

"And on that note, ma'am, some sort of issue happened with the alert schedule. We have the ship, but the listed alert unit is on the other side of the system."

"I'm going to literally murder someone. Response time?"

"At least four hours."

Bryn pinched the bridge of her nose. "Who else do we have that's colocated with the alert dropship? Array seizure capable."

Obin pushed the roster and schedule over to Bryn on the shipnet. She scanned through it, her eyes flickering back and forth. She stopped suddenly.

"There. Raven Zero-One is prepping for a training mission. Have them switch to live ordnance and get them to the dropship." Her finger hovered over the glowing outline of *Second Company*. "What do you know about them? Where do their loyalties lie?"

Obin nodded as she spoke. "I'm familiar with that particular unit. We sent them to the Obershire exchange for security some years back. Their commander is... many things, but he's always been loyal to the Executor. To you, now."

"Good. See that he knows where the orders are coming from, and I want updates as soon as you have them. Alert all elements of the fleet that are in-system as well; if this goes poorly, we need to be ready."

31

IN WHICH THERE ARE WARRIORS

And then the giant rose, his eyes the
Stones of the shore, his breath the salt
And the spray that crashed—and he spoke
You stand on the shore of the Well

Björn Hafthor was not a small man. His mother and father had always wondered where his height came from. Björn had towered above them before he was twelve. Now standing on the raised platform with his squad seated in the briefing room in front of him, he seemed an absolute giant. The scowl that knit his bushy eyebrows together completed the illusion.

"Cortez, shut the fuck up and listen. It's a training mission, but you know what we're getting ready for. The real shit is just around the corner, and I need you to kindly unfuck yourself."

Cortez swallowed her smile. "Sure, boss. Sorry."

Björn turned back to the wall, where the hand-drawn diagram displayed the target training complex on the asteroid. "As Cortez has so cleverly pointed out, I'm drawing on the fucking wall like a neanderthal. This is a low-tech op. Your suit systems will be suspended in the software, and you'll be limited to tightbeam only. Yes, that means you wanna talk you have to aim your comm laser by hand." The groans were only scattered. Better.

"Insertion is via assault pod, two by two. Pods will be considered a loss, so if you have to crack them go for it. However, our supply wonks wanted me to pass on that they would greatly appreciate not having to requisition a full new complement of pods." Björn tapped the red X on each corner of the complex.

"Blocking positions here and here, that'll be Charlie and Delta. Alpha, you've got breach. Bravo's outer cordon." Cortez groaned. Björn ignored her.

At this, a thin man chewing on a small piece of wire like a toothpick grinned slightly, muttering, "Fuck yeah, bout time…" Like Cortez, Chetachi was an immigrant to Ollson space, rare but not unheard of. His father had moved from Adebe territory looking for work. He'd always enjoyed the tales of his father's work in the forges, and when he had the opportunity to enlist in the Ollson forces, his specialty was obvious—demolition. The small detonator wire was inert this time. Björn hoped.

Björn continued outlining the mission briefing, his eyes moving to each team leader in the room as he handed out tasks and discussed support plans for casualties, simulated naval fire support, and eventual extraction. After he finished describing the last phase, he turned back to the group. Alena and Cortez had finished writing, their arms crossed as they looked at the diagram on the wall. They were two of his sharpest team leaders.

"All right. Any saved rounds or reattacks before we go kit up?" Sure enough, Alena raised her chin at Björn, and he nodded back.

"If we mana—" The room was suddenly lit red, a klaxon blaring in the hallway.

Alert. Björn clapped his hands sharply in the sudden din. "Kit up, let's fucking *move* people!"

"We're not even on the fucking schedule. What's up with this?" Alena's voice barely made it over the noise as she ran. Björn ignored her as he moved behind her toward the door.

His team leaders were ahead of him. He followed them down the hallways to the team room, where the klaxon was somehow louder. Thumping of suited boots already filled the air, and the slap and crack of weapons prep cut across the low rumble. Björn's chest swelled with pride at how far along they were. *Second Company, first to the fight.* His troops were the best that the 409th Tactical Reconnaissance Regiment had to offer and had the battle streamers to prove it. Not just those from the Mendicant Wars either. The newest and brightest came from their actions repelling Revenant forces trying to raid Osman warehouses.

Björn sprinted to his locker, keying his suit with his implants along the way. It stepped out of the storage configuration and split down the front, each arm and leg folding open to reveal the soft pink inside like some obscene and deadly flower. He tossed his overclothes into the back of the locker and pressed the seal on his skinsuit down before stepping into the combat suit, its display coming to life as the helmet snapped down over his head. System startup was already complete, and he felt the suit come alive, the slightly unsettling feeling of wires welding at the base of his spine. He could feel every thruster, cannon, reactor, and active armor plate like a wearable tank. His command suit was relatively lightly armed but heavily armored, with multiple shielded and redundant comm arrays.

Björn stepped out of the staging area quickly but without sprinting. It would be easy to inadvertently damage something on the hangar deck by running in the suit—or, more importantly, someone. An unarmored soldier was terrifyingly vulnerable.

Across the bay, the ground crew hurried to detach fuel service hoses and dog the hatches on the outside of the rapid response vehicle. Its bulbous fuselage curved away as Björn stationed himself at the rear ramp for the headcount. While he could see the exact whereabouts of each of his soldiers on his helmet display, he preferred to get a measure of the Ravens of the Second face to face as they boarded. It helped them to see him there as they embarked, his red command flash the color of fresh blood on his gauntlets. *Leaders should be seen.*

The soldiers looked ready, if somewhat nervous. His HUD ticked the time-since-alert in angry red, the glowing numbers superimposed over the view through his visor. The soldiers were not all aboard; it looked like one was still back at the kit lockers. Grunting in annoyance, he keyed the command net.

"Attention on the net, we are four-plus-thirty and counting. Raven Two-One, say status."

Cortez's voice came back, all business now. "Raven Zero-One, Raven Two-One, Raven Two-One Whiskey has a suit malf. Stuck in start loop. I've called maintenance."

"Two-One, Zero-One, we don't have time for this. I'm passing green to the flight deck. Link up with One-One for cyber coverage."

"Zero-One, Two-One, wilco." If Cortez had a weakness, it was that she was too focused on perfection. Better to get to the fight quickly and be down one body than to get there too late. *She should know better.* Björn turned as Cortez followed the last functional soldier onto the ship and looked for one of the pilots. The pilots were unarmored but wore basic survival suits with fat plugs in the lower back for the ship interface. They didn't like having to step their way around the massive, armored soldiers, so they waited until the deck was clear before moving in to complete their final exterior checks.

The crew commander clambered up the ladder to the cockpit as her second pilot walked quickly around the ship, his eyes following a pointing finger as he banged the hatches he could reach to check that they were secure. Björn waited impatiently at the ramp, forcing himself to breathe slowly and steadily. He actually did want the second pilot to do a thorough job, despite Björn's nearly overwhelming urge to *go.* Finally, after a terse thumbs-up echoed back to the pilot, he swung up into the rear and stepped back into his cradle. His second in command, Axen Troub, was already strapped in, the red and gold XO insignia gleaming dully on their chest plate. Troub greeted him with a feral grin. At least they looked as excited as he felt.

He felt his stomach lurch as the ship lifted off, and he keyed over to the common band. It was already rife with chatter, and no wonder. It wasn't often that a live alert came in. Time to shut everyone up.

Björn took a breath, then bellowed, "*Second Company!*"

A scattered response as only a few people heard him. "First to fight!"

"Is that all the more you've got, *hugleysingjar*? I said *Second company!*"

This time the response made his suit key the volume down.
"First to fight!"
"That's more like it. This is a live alert, not an elaborate training drill. Check your suits now for full authority and ensure you have live ordnance; I don't want any stupid mistakes. Orders came with the Executor's personal seal, so don't fuck up. XO, your brief." While he had been getting the headcount and checking with the ship's crew, Troub had spent the time reviewing the mission details—what few there were. The file was suspiciously small.

"Yes, sir." Their voice was crisp and snappy. Traub had a cool head, and Björn had never seen them riled. "We have a breach in security at the fold array." An audible gasp on the net was clipped off. "The array has not yet been activated, so we believe the security algorithms are holding their own for now, at least in the array control core. Obviously, the source code won't be affected, but if we lose core control our mission will become much different." *Ah,* thought Björn, *that's why they needed a full recon company.* Traub continued, "We have at least one enemy agent, appears female, below-average height, last seen here." An image of a woman in black maintenance clothing crouched at an access panel leaped up in their shared visual space. "We have no comms with the array inhabitants. Exterior imagery shows the majority of airlocks open. It's safe to assume those who made it to a suit are staying put. Standard protocol is to hunker down, so we can consider all movers hostile." Their voice ended on a clipped, sure note. "That's all for the brief."

Björn had been reviewing the fold array schematics while Traub spoke and saw the rest of his team lead glyphs in the file with him. It didn't look like there had been any substantive changes to hardware or arrangement since their last exercise for a fold array scenario. "All players, Raven Zero-One. Two objectives. One, secure the core and purge any foreign code. I want that thing scraped back to the source; as long as we keep containment, we can rewrite it. Two, secure the fold mouth. If we fail on one, we can assume the array will activate and whoever is waiting on the other side really wants to come through. Overlapping fields of fire but keep your declination angles at least thirty degrees; I don't want a stray round damaging the array." He paused, chewing his lip. Cortez's team was down a cyber soldier. That made the laydown decision easy if not ideal. "We're going with epsilon standard maneuvers. Alpha and Bravo, you're on exterior kinetic clear and objective two. Call secure on command net." He heard the Chetachi and Cortez, the Alpha and Bravo team leaders, acknowledge with a few short clicks, and saw the comm lines to their teams light up green in his HUD as they started issuing orders. "Charlie and Delta, set blocking positions on the airlocks and infil for cyber and objective one." He saw the soldiers facing him from Delta nod behind their armored visors, and his HUD blipped a green assent glyph from Alena and Svon. "I don't want anyone inside until we know the software status. Expect everything to be compromised except the core, so full hostile systems. We will be emission condition zero." He paused for a moment. "And that does mean EMCON Zero. You all know what the sensor suite is on the array. The last thing we want is to show up like an EM billboard. Any questions." Björn paused for a few beats, hearing nothing on the net. "Okay, we are twelve mikes out, released for team planning."

He keyed over to the intra-ship net. He saw the soldiers across from him blank their visors, retreating into the shared tactical space of the troop network. He would join them in a moment to watch the details of the plan come together, but first, he needed to check with the crew commander.

"Crew commander, Raven Zero-One."

The response was immediate. "*Skítur*, Björn, figured you assholes would be the baggage on my alert watch."

Björn grinned at the familiar voice. "Well, shoot, I guess I don't have to worry about a damn thing now that we got Captain Gotesdottir, Fist of the Empress, Slayer of Monsters, and generally steely-eyed combat pilot driving."

"Shut the fuck up, Björn. I'm trying to calculate a decel burn that won't turn you into soup in a can. I don't have the two spare brain cells it would take to spar with you."

"Good to hear your voice, Cap. I'll let you know when we have a requested insertion vector."

"You too, snugglebear. Better snap fuckin to it. We're gonna flip and burn in four plus thirty, and then you're gonna land wherever I put you."

"Roger that." Björn smiled and shook his head. Snugglebear. The impudence. He could snap her like a twig. Björn dropped into the shared troop net to see where they were with the planning.

32

IN WHICH THERE MAY BE COMBAT

The troop ship braked. *Hard.*
Björn saw every soldier's suit lock up in crash position, their cradles rotating as the ship gyrated wildly. An unpredictable approach vector was one thing, but this was downright crazy. He cursed silently to himself. His jaw locked shut against the gravities. As the pressure mounted, he felt himself straining more and more, the suit squeezing his lower body to force the blood back toward his head. *Those Rassgat pilots,* he thought, *snug and probably fucking comfortable in their gel.*

He'd been involved in an attempt to integrate the acceleration gel into drop soldier's suits, making them able to withstand more battering. It wasn't a new idea; some variation of the program went back as far as he'd felt like scrolling in the Ollson archives one night. And it still didn't work. A soldier couldn't wait while the fluid drained, and the armor didn't give them everything they needed. Sometimes you had to *see* what you were shooting at, not just blindly follow the HUD overlay and sensor feeds. Pilots really did have it easy.

When the drop light finally switched to amber, Björn was barely holding on to consciousness. He keyed a nonverbal alert to his team leads and watched the board green up. Everyone was ready, and when the giant hand on his chest finally disappeared, he gasped. The drop light switched to green, and he felt his cradle begin a swift acceleration toward the nose of the ship. *High aspect insertion, what the fuck, Gotesdottir? You better not have fu—* and his cradle whipped around the end of the launching rail, and he was out, tail-end soldier in a spread of night-dark suits ripping through the void toward the fold array. With his suit on complete electromagnetic lockdown, he couldn't see a single one of them. He just had to hope that Gotesdottir had hit her mark.

The fold array rushed toward him, a diabolical doughnut of metal superstructure and nightmarish spines. Even having trained to take one of these over and over, in sim and in person, Björn was never able to shake the unutterable *strangeness* of them. He threw off the feeling. Time to go to work.

The glowing line painted by his suit showed him on target. The perfect spot for a command element, near the top of a low protrusion with good line of sight to two of the four airlocks. The defense cannon might still be able to reach him, but those were less of a concern once he got down safely. They were designed to fire outward, which put him in the firing line for now.

The doughnut grew closer, now nearly filling his view. He hadn't seen any fire yet. That was a good sign. Then he saw a flash of light to his right, about where Alpha should have been close to retro fire and deceleration. It didn't look like suit jets slowing to land. Björn knew a suit frag when he saw one.

His onboard AI highlighted the movement just to the right of his intended landing point. A single defense maser jived and tracked, its barrel gripped between two elbow-jointed servo arms that maneuvered it, whiplike, toward the incoming troopers. They were blown. Björn keyed the general net.

"Attention on the net, weapons red!" The shared net roared to life around him as his soldiers relaxed their emissions discipline. Radar, lidar, datalinks, tightbeam bursts tore through the once-quiescent spectrum. The jammers went up first, washing out the main comm band used by the array radios. A moment later, the transmitters disappeared in a shower of liquid metal. Björn saw the defense maser still moving and tracking as another of his soldiers flared and died to his left.

"Charlie, check zap for target, my laser mark, one by razorback." He lined up the indicator for his wrist-mounted targeting laser on the defense turret, his helmet showing him the shine of strong return from the offending beam weapon. A moment later, he heard Cortez's voice.

"Tally."

"Cleared to engage."

"Weapon away, ten seconds." He saw the telemetry from the guided missile pop up in his visor, arcing toward the defense cannon. The cannon noticed the incoming missile and whipped around to point at the threat, nearly disappearing under a cloud of chaff. The tiny pieces of mirrored foil bounced and diffused his laser mark, and he saw the missile waver and slow its engine slightly as it sought to re-acquire. Too late, and it flared a tiny bloom of death as the defense cannon returned to tracking the incoming soldiers. The entire sequence had taken only about twenty seconds; they still had nearly a minute until the last soldier would land on the array. *Can't afford to let this thing pick us off.*

"Charlie, Delta, re-attack, same mark, same target. Request simultaneous impacts." He kept the designator on the beam cannon, now emerged from the haze of foil chaff.

"Charlie tally." The call was immediate.

A few seconds later. "Delta tally."

"Cleared to engage." This time he saw two blooms of data in his visor from left and right. He couldn't afford too many more misses; they didn't carry a lot of heavy ordnance, and he had no idea what internal defensive systems were corrupted. The same sequence of chaff, waiver, kill, but this time the second missile whipped in under the metallic cloud and slammed into the defense cannon. He let out a satisfied whoop, and then it was time to focus on decelerating. *Gonna want to stick this landing.*

The array came crashing toward him. His sky, once wide and clear, now had a metal horizon. He twisted and flipped feet-first, looking down. The range ticked down in his HUD. At a terrifyingly small number, his suit jet kicked him in the lower back, and then his boots hit the metal, clamping tightly. Alpha and Bravo called, "Positions set," immediately after he touched down.

Traub had set up on the other side of the array ring, their tightbeam keeping a solid connection with his. Both his and the XO's command suits emitted a steady stream of microdrones, simple comm relays that glittered with density around the shoulder dispensers, then faded as they dispersed. The two command suits looked like night-dark demons, their onyx wings fading into space.

The cyber soldiers called contact with the array, and he saw their firewalls clang up almost immediately. It was standard protocol to isolate themselves from the rest of the unit while they fought for information dominance, but usually he was otherwise occupied with the more physical side of combat. It felt weird, just waiting for them to work, but only one enemy agent was inside and no point in risking lives to compromised systems. Hell, even the emergency blast doors could be weaponized; he'd seen the Revenants drop a particularly nasty virus into an Obershire refinery that waited a full month before carefully cutting the crew into pieces as they passed the blast door thresholds.

He fired off a quick situation report to brigade HQ, his suit boosting the signal enough to make it to the nearest relay. It wasn't much to report; positions set, conducting software clear. He mostly just wanted to keep them from asking too many questions and getting in his way; no good would come from some fatass general trying to run things with a ten-minute lightspeed lag.

Finally, the cybers came back on the troop net. "We're clear to press in, but we'll need to hard wipe each node drive as we come to it. The core is pretty well on lockdown; no one is going to fold in or out until we can re-flash the firmware." Good news all around then. *Still, don't get cocky.*

"All right, Alpha and Bravo, you're approved breach. Watch your sectors. I want webs out on any turrets you see. We are going to flush this spy out if we have to search every locker by hand. I want her alive. Cortez, that means *able to answer questions*. Brain-dead counts as dead."

Cortez's grin carried through the comms. "Aww shoot, Cap, you know I won't kill her. Loud and clear."

33

IN WHICH STRANGE THINGS ARE FOUND

―

Björn had grunted at the irony when he got the call. The search took two hours, but they finally found the woman who had caused all the trouble. She was folded up into a topologically unlikely size in a storage locker. Cortez's team had made the capture, managing to get a stunner on her.

Now, Björn stood just outside the airlock where three soldiers clustered around the woman. She was still unconscious, her wrists bound behind her back and face down toward the deck. The airlock was fitting for a field interrogation; any misbehavior could be swiftly dealt with. Alpha's cyber team finished their physical scans, and Kendrick, the team leader, moved down the corridor to where Björn and Troub stood with the four platoon leaders. He dialed down the tint on his helmet as he moved, revealing his round, jovial face.

He smiled warmly at them all before speaking on the command net. "*Fjandinn hafi það*, Cap. Where the fuck did this come from? This bitch is fucking loaded to the tits. Onboard hardware you could run a large cruiser with, and her fucking physical mods encompass what I would term weird shit." Björn raised an eyebrow. "Yeah, she's not fucking wired or anything. Don't worry about that, but she's got fucking I/O jacks and wetware ports near every major nerve cluster. If she ever fucking plugged them all in at once, she'd be embedded like a gods damned spider. Deep black-ops fuckery for sure."

Björn suppressed a grimace at the profanity. "That your professional opinion, then?"

"Fuckin-A, sir."

"Thank you. That'll be all." Kendrick grinned again, gave a sharp salute, and returned to the still-unconscious woman. Björn and his leadership group followed. The cyber troops standing by the spy looked back at Björn expectantly.

Björn keyed the company net. "All right. Let's find out what she knows. Wake her up." As one of the soldiers reached out with a shock stick, the woman flipped over to stare at him, her face deadpan.

The soldier's voice boomed out of the speakers of his suit. "Identify yourself." The woman looked from one to the other and then took a deep breath. She held it, her eyes rolling back in her head. Her skin, once pale, began to darken. The cyber soldiers looked at each other and then jumped back almost simultaneously. One slammed the airlock controls, and the inner doors scissored shut. A glow was just visible through the small window.

Björn ran forward, elbowing one of the soldiers out of the way to get a look. The woman lay on the floor, her bones glowing through her skin, mouth gaping. He heard, almost felt, a deep vibration come through the decking and into his suit. The light coming from the woman became brighter, and Björn slapped the emergency outer airlock door release. The outer door snapped open, blowing her out into the vacuum. He glimpsed her there, mouth still open with the blazing light pouring out of it, and then his visor gained down, and he was momentarily blind. The gentle rain of whatever was left of the woman made a soft sound on the airlock door like a million little fingers tapping at the metal.

Björn looked at Traub, whose mouth was still open behind the visor, their normally calm demeanor visibly shaken. Björn keyed the private channel to Traub.

"Any idea what the fuck just happened?"

"No, Cap. Right now, for some reason, all I can think of is this's gonna be one weird-ass report."

"We aren't writing that into a fucking report. Run the cyber team personally. See what you can get out of whatever is left. I'm going to debrief the station head, and then we'll figure out how to report this. I feel like the normal chain of command isn't going to be a good place to drop this ball of shit right now."

"Yes, sir."

■■■

Bryn's eyes flicked over the preliminary report. It had come encrypted to her key, the recon company commander's terse writing now flowing across her vision. *At least he's not given to conjecture.* The report was concise. He had even included estimates from his cyber element on how long the re-imaging of the array would take. While she would have been disappointed at their absence, she was impressed that a low-level field commander had thought to include the information she needed to make strategic decisions. *Perhaps Captain Hafthor would be better suited reporting directly to me.* That would, at the very least, keep him farther from the influence of the admiralty.

Bryn closed the report and her eyes, her fingers moving to massage her temples. She would have to go back into the archives to find the last time a spy had tried to gain access to an Ollson fold array. Probably to the crypt to talk to anyone who even remembered such a thing. And now here she was, alone at the head of the great Geneline Ollson, and the enemies were already at the gates. She had no idea how the Obershire spy had managed to get past the network security that quickly or how she had managed that neat trick of suicide.

Ollson spies were, of course, issued kill software to be used in the event of capture, but they didn't have the high-energy implants of an Executor. Even then, the energy output of the woman on the array had been an order of magnitude higher than what should have been possible. Bryn's implants held significant stored energy and recharged from her motion. But they wouldn't be enough to blow a hole in the side of an array. Even though Captain Hafthor had sent her out the airlock, the woman's detonation had melted off antennas and damaged the array for hundreds of meters.

Bryn's eyes snapped open, and she stood, walking around her desk to the large window that overlooked the rest of Karvasok station. The tiers, rounded and studded with windows and antennae, cascaded down to the main docking section where the *Sleipnir* lay berthed, a massive dark octopus in a diamond cradle. The ship was a thoroughbred, built for war in a time long since past. It had served the Geneline Ollson for three Executors, and now had passed into Bryn's hands. It was good to see it there, a reminder of where the Ollson future lay. War was coming, Bryn knew, and the spy was only the beginning.

She turned away from the window, calling up the queue of combat simulations the admiralty had sent her. It was time to cast off any illusions that her father might somehow come charging into the rescue with a full imperial pardon. She had no idea where Erick was or when she'd see him again. But the spy proved the enemy was here, and while she might have years until ships met in combat, one thing was for certain.

The war was on.

Don't miss Iron on the Tongue, Reckoning Book 2!

Sign Up

Read More Stories

www.ingramcontent.com/pod-product-compliance
Lightning Source LLC
LaVergne TN
LVHW041630060526
838200LV00040B/1519